ORGANIZING to COLLABORATE

A Taxonomy of Higher Education Practices for Promoting Interdependence Within the Classroom, Across the Campus, and Beyond the College

Joseph B. Cuseo

Marymount College

NEW FORUMS
Stillwater, Oklahoma
U.S.A.

This book may be ordered in bulk quantities at discount from New Forums Press, Inc., P.O. Box 876, Stillwater, OK 74076 [Federal I.D. No. 73 1123239]. Printed in the United States of America.

International Standard Book Number: 1-58107-045-4

Contents

Section I.
Introduction to the Taxonomy

Purposes of the Taxonomy

The terms "collaborative learning," "cooperative learning," and "learning community" have been bandied about in American higher education with great frequency and enthusiasm. Unfortunately, these terms have a long history of being inconsistently defined, both conceptually and operationally, resulting in their being used interchangeably by some educators and differentially by others (Hord, 1981). After reviewing the higher education literature, Chickerking and Gamson (1987) concluded that these terms are far more "commodious" than they are precise. More recently, Pat Cross (1998) concluded that there is still considerable "debate" over the definition of these terms, and Brower and Dettinger (1998) contend that they have become so widely used, for so many different types of programs and activities, that they are now on the verge of becoming a "trendy buzzword."

One primary purpose of this monograph is to provide a more precise delineation of postsecondary practices that are subsumed or assumed to be embraced by the umbrella terms, collaborative learning, cooperative learning, and learning community, and organize these practices into a coherent classification system or taxonomy. Other major objectives of the taxonomy are to: (a) create a common *language* for improving the *clarity* of communication and discourse about diverse forms of collaboration in higher education; (b) articulate a

---

strong, *research-based rationale* for greater use of collaborative practices in postsecondary education, (c) provide a panoramic *overview* of, and a convenient *catalogue* for, the wide range of collaborative initiatives that have been implemented at colleges and universities; and (d) serve as a *stimulus* for triggering *wider use* of collaborative practices in higher education.

Organization of the Taxonomy

The etymological root of the term *collaboration* is "co-labor," which literally means "to labor together." Thus, collaboration may be conceptually defined as a *social (interpersonal)* relationship in which *two or more individuals work interdependently* in a manner that is both *mutually supportive* and *reciprocally beneficial*—i.e., both parties *give* something and *get* something. Collaborative educational practices are distinguished by their lack of individualism and competitiveness, and their high degree of positive interdependence among the persons involved.

Using the foregoing conceptual definition as a starting point, *collaborative educational practices* will be adopted as the generic, overarching rubric for the proposed taxonomy. The specific nature of the *persons involved* in the collaborative process is used as the key criterion for differentiating collaborative educational practices into *seven* major categories: (1) collaboration between *students*, (2) collaboration between *faculty*, (3) collaboration between *faculty and students*, (4) *cross-functional* teams—i.e., collaboration between members of different professional divisions or functional units within the college, (5) *inter-institutional* collaboration between different undergraduate institutions, (6) *inter-segmental* collaboration across different segments or sectors of the educational system—elementary through graduate/professional school, and (7) *college-community* collaboration, i.e., collaboration between colleges and other institutions, organizations, or members of the community outside of the educational system (for example, businesses and public service organizations).

Within these seven major categories, particular subcategories or subtypes of collaboration are identified and described. In effect, the general categories represent the *who* of it—the persons involved in the collaborative process, and the specific subcategories represent the *how* of it—the procedural strategies used to engender collaboration among the persons involved. For the purpose of providing a quick and convenient overview of the taxonomy's general organization, a skeletal outline of its structure is listed below. The complete taxonomy, including research-based support for all categories and detailed descriptions of illustrative practices, is included in Section II of this monograph.

1. COLLABORATION BETWEEN *STUDENTS*

1.1 *Small Group Discussions (a.k.a., "Buzz Groups")*

1.2 *Group Projects/Group Reports*

1.3 *Study Groups*
• *Test-Preparation* Groups
• *Note-Taking* Groups
• *Reading* Groups
• *Library Research* Groups
• *Test-Results Review* Groups
• *Group Conferences with the Instructor*

1.4 *Collaborative Learning*

1.5 *Cooperative Learning*
- *Paining* Structures: *Dyadic* (*Two*-Member) Teams
- *Small-Group* Structures: 3-4 Member Teams
- Structures Explicitly Designed to Promote *Positive Interdependence*
- Structures Explicitly Designed To Promote *Individual Accountability*
- Structures Designed To Facilitate *Team Formation*
- Structures Designed To Promote *Between-Team Interaction* and *Whole-Class Synergy*

1.6 *Problem-Based Learning (PBL)*

1.7 *Guided Design*

1.8 *Learning Communities*
- *Course-Linking Models*
- *Learning Clusters*
- *Freshman Interest Groups (FIGs)*
- *Interest Groups in the Major* (a.k.a., *Junior Interest Groups*)
- *Federated Learning Communities (FLCs)*
- *Coordinated Studies Programs*

1.9 *Cluster Colleges* (a.k.a., *Colleges-Within-A-College Program*)

1.10 *Peer Teaching-Learning Programs*:
- *Peer Tutoring*
- *Supplemental Instruction (SI)*
- *Writing Fellows*

1.11 *Peer Mentoring Programs*

---

4. COLLABORATIVE ***CROSS-FUNCTIONAL TEAMS***
(Collaboration Between Members of Different
Functional Units or Professional Divisions
Within the College)

4.1 *Educational Partnerships between the Divisions of*
Academic Affairs & Student Life

4.2 *Educational Partnerships between **Classroom
Instructors** & **Academic Support*** Services

4.3 *Cross-Functional **Committees**, **Task Forces, &
Conference Teams***

5. ***INTER-INSTITUTIONAL*** COLLABORATION
(Collaboration Between Undergraduate Institutions)

5.1 Collaboration between ***2-year*** & ***4-year*** Institutions

5.2 Collaboration among ***4-year*** Institutions

6. ***INTER-SEGMENTAL*** COLLABORATION
(Collaboration Across Different Segments or Sectors
of the Educational System)

6.1 Collaboration between ***Schools (Elementary or
Secondary) & Colleges***, a.k.a., ***School-College
Partnerships***

6.2 Collaboration between ***Undergraduate Colleges*** &
Graduate/Professional Schools

---

7. **COLLEGE-COMMUNITY** COLLABORATION
(Collaboration Between Colleges and Corporations,
Non-Profit Organizations, or Citizens in the Local
Community)

    7.1 Collaboration between *Colleges* and **Corporate Organizations**

    7.2 Collaboration between *Colleges* and **Non-Profit Organizations** *or* **Citizens in the** Local Community

Limitations of the Taxonomy

The categories comprising the taxonomy are not mutually exclusive, so a practice listed in one category may contain elements that could qualify it for inclusion in a different category. Some collaborative practices are multifaceted, embracing a number of distinct components, so it was necessary to cross-list them in more than one category. Final decisions about the categorical placement of particular practices were based on what the author perceived to be the practice's most salient procedural pattern or purpose.

An attempt was made to construct a typology that was both inclusive and comprehensive. However, the number of collaborative procedures cited in the taxonomy is by no means exhaustive; there are undoubtedly other noteworthy forms of collaboration that have not been enumerated or illustrated within the proposed classification system. It is also acknowledged that the taxonomy represents only one of many possible classificatory schemes, so it is not offered as a definitive framework, but merely as a working model or heuristic to help guide, organize, and facilitate collaborative efforts.

Feedback from readers is welcomed regarding major forms of collaboration in higher education that may have been over-looked or omitted.

Rationale for the Taxonomy

Beginning in the 1980's, an educational reform move-ment emerged in America that was ignited by a spate of scath-ing national reports on the status of higher education (Asso-ciation of American Colleges, 1985, 1988; Boyer, 1987; Edu-cation Commission of the States, 1986; National Endowment for the Humanities, 1984; National Institute of Education, 1984; Wingspread Group, 1993). This reform movement was fueled subsequently by national concerns over institutional assessment, accountability, and quality that surfaced within a national climate of economic retrenchment and cost cutting (El-Khawas, 1987; Ewell & Boyer, 1998; Orfield, 1993). A recurrent theme in virtually all the reform reports is a clarion call for more "connections" between (a) students, (b) faculty, (c) disciplines, (d) colleges and schools, and (e) academic and experiential learning.

A comprehensive response to the full spectrum of issues raised by the reform movement requires diverse forms col-laboration among a wide range of constituents, working both inside and outside of higher education. Consensus is emerg-ing among educational reform agents that "single-shot fixes" are not working (Haylock, 1996); instead, concerted, multi-faceted efforts are seen as having the collective potential to exert synergistic effects that lead to systemic and enduring change. As the late Ernest Boyer (1992) once said, the key to promoting positive, long-term reform in higher education is for its constituents to convert their "little loyalties" into "larger loyalties," and work as "creative cooperators" rather than "conforming competitors."

Engagement in creative, comprehensive collaborative practice seems essential if higher education expects to redress its historical weaknesses and respond effectively to its current challenges. Consider the following eight issues that perennially challenge American higher education and how each could be better met if colleges and universities made more use of the collaborative strategies described in the proposed taxonomy.

1. The challenge of promoting students' *active involvement* and *personal responsibility* in the learning process.

This challenge could be better met if college faculty were to rely less on traditional, instructor-centered lectures and made more use of *collaborative and cooperative learning*—pedagogical practices that place *students* at the center of the learning experience. Learner-centered pedagogy increases students' level of involvement and sense of personal responsibility for their own learning by actively engaging them with the subject matter and with other learners (McKeachie, Pintrich, Lin, & Smith, 1986).

2. The challenge of promoting *student retention*, i.e., student *persistence* to course and program *completion*.

The institutional retention (graduation) rate of college students in America is less than 50% (Tinto, 1993). Retention in science and math courses and degree programs is particularly low among student populations who are underrepresented in these fields—such as females, African-Americans, and Hispanics (Minorities in the Sciences, 1994;

Tobias, 1990; Treisman in Green, 1989). Adoption of *cooperative-learning* pedagogies and *learning-community* curricular structures could provide these learners with the peer support and social integration that are known to contribute significantly to student retention (Pascarella & Terenzini, 1991).

Curriculum-focused, *classroom*-based collaboration may also be critical for ensuring peer interaction and social integration among the large and rising number of *commuter* and *part-time* students attending college (Levine & Cureton, 1998). These students are at risk for attrition because their commuting and off-campus work commitments prevent them from developing retention-promoting networks on campus via the traditional channels of extracurricular (co-curricular) experiences and involvement in campus life (Astin, 1993). Thus, provision of "intra-curricular" opportunities for peer interaction and social bonding among commuters may be a potent compensatory strategy for promoting their social integration into the college community and reducing their high risk for attrition (Gabelnick, MacGregor, Matthews, & Smith, 1990).

3. The challenge of promoting *coherence in the curriculum*.

The undergraduate curriculum has been criticized repeatedly for being *fragmented, disjointed* and *incoherent*. In particular, the *general education* component of the college curriculum has been characterized as a dizzying array of "distribution requirements" which are taken "smorgasbord style"— a little of this and a little of that with little sense of connection among general education courses (*breadth* requirements), or connection between general education courses and specific courses in the student's major (*depth* requirements). At some colleges and universities, general education requirements may actually be fulfilled by taking a variety of very narrowly-focused, esoteric courses which represent the specialized research interests of the faculty rather than a true "core" curriculum—i.e., courses that every educated college graduate should experience because of their pervasive relevance for all humans and all careers (Association of American Colleges, 1985; National Endowment for the Humanities, 1984).

Collaboration among students and faculty involved in *interdisciplinary* learning communities may forge meaningful connections across the curriculum, providing a potential antidote to the increasing hyper-specialization of academic professions and the growing isolation of academic disciplines (Association of American Colleges, 1988). Interdisciplinary courses and cross-disciplinary teaching teams can also foster a sense of community among the college faculty and promote a sense of common purpose among different academic divisions or departments within the college (Association of American Colleges, 1990).

4. The challenge of *unifying the curriculum and co-curriculum*.

For approximately 25 years, the higher education literature has pointed to a "persistent gap" or "schism" between the formal (academic) curriculum and the co-curriculum—i.e., student development programming outside the classroom (American College Personnel Association, 1994; Miller and Prince, 1976). Some disturbing consequences of this schism have been (a) rigid compartmentalization of professional responsibilities into the offices of "academic" or "student" affairs, (b) divisive territorial politics and dysfunctional competition for resources between these two major units of the college (Kuh & Banta, 2000), and (c) splintering of students' liberal education and holistic development into disjointed parts (Barr & Upcraft, 1990).

Collaborative partnerships between *academic and student development* professionals can help close the persistent gap that now exists between the formal curriculum and the co-curriculum. Collaborative relations between the divisions of academic and student affairs may serve to unite members of the college community who have been historically and artificially separated by organizational or functional boundaries.such collaboration could also lay the foundation for mutually productive partnerships between academic and student development professionals that can simultaneously promote their own professional development and their students' holistic development. As Ernest Boyer argues, "A college of quality has goals that are greater than the sum of the separate parts and reminds students in formal and informal ways, that there is an intellectual and social community to which they are inextricably connected" (1987, p. 286).

Furthermore, higher education research reveals that (a) colleges with high morale have a campus culture that is perceived by faculty and staff as being more collaborative than competitive or individualistic (Austin, Rice, Splete, & Associates, 1991), and (b) student retention is more effectively promoted at institutions where there is collaboration between academic and student affairs (Kuh, Schuh, Whitt, & Associates, 1991; Stodt, & Klepper, 1987).

5. The challenge of promoting and appreciating ethnical and racial *diversity*.

Greater collaboration between *schools* (elementary and secondary) and colleges has, as one of its many possible byproducts, the potential for improving the access and success of underrepresented students through (a) earlier educational intervention, (b) better academic preparation of students for college, and (c) more targeted recruitment of students to college.

Also, greater inter-segmental collaboration between *2-year* and *4-year* colleges should facilitate the "vertical" transfer of minority students, 50% of whom begin higher education at community colleges (Carter & Wilson, 1995); in fact, more first-generation minority students are enrolled at community colleges than at all of our nation's 4-year colleges and universities combined (California Community Colleges, 1994). This represents a sizable pool of under-represented students who could potentially transfer to 4-year colleges and eventually reap the well-documented benefits associated with the completion of a baccalaureate degree (Pascarella & Terenzini, 1991).

Unfortunately, the 2- to 4-year college transfer rate for minority students remains significantly lower than majority students (Barrera & Angel, 1991; Rendon & Garza, 1996), despite the fact that minority students have equally high aspirations for the baccalaureate degree (Center for the Study of Community Colleges, 1985; London, 1996). Even at urban community colleges, at least half of the enrolled minority students entertain aspirations for the baccalaureate degree (Richardson & Bender, 1987). As Rendon and Garza note: "While community colleges have sought to find their niche in postsecondary education by concentrating on career-based education to prepare students to enter the job market, many educators are concerned that higher expectations should be set for students of color, particularly since minorities occupy few privileged positions in society in which undergraduate degree are necessary" (1996, p. 290).

Among under-represented students who have been recruited to college, *learning community* programs can promote their retention and academic achievement through block scheduling and enrollment in the same cluster of courses. This curricular practice can provide at-risk students with a retention-promoting cohort of peers, and a common schedule conducive to out-of-class study groups—the formation of which has been found to exert a significant salutary effect on the academic achievement of under-represented students (Treisman, 1985; Bonsangue, 1993).

While in class, *cooperative learning* techniques can ensure that minority and majority students have well-structured opportunities for constructive interaction, positive interdependence, and joint pursuit of common goals. These are social conditions that have been found to be most effective for reducing racial prejudice and promoting harmonious interracial relations (Amir, 1969; McConahay, 1981; Worchel, 1979).

6. The challenge of integrating the *college experience* and the *world of work*.

Student learning in higher education has bee criticized for lacking connections (a) between courses, (b) between courses and the co-curriculum, and (c) between the collegiate experience and the work world (Gardner & Lambert, 1993; Holton, 1995). Partnerships between professional members of the college community and corporate professionals who employ college graduates may serve to bridge the gap between college and career and reduce the "job shock" often experienced by college graduates (Leibowitz, Schlossberg, & Shore; Taylor, 1988). Faculty could team with business leaders in corporate organizations to identify behaviors or skills possessed by college graduates that are most closely associated with effective career performance. Faculty and employers of college graduates might collaborate further to develop college students' professional performance skills and career-success strategies before they enter the work world (Lasher & Brush, 1990).

College-corporate partnerships may also serve to promote a more harmonious, symbiotic relationship between the college and its surrounding community. This is a desirable end in itself because it serves to improve college-community ("town-gown") relations. Furthermore, it may serve to lay the groundwork needed for securing student internships in general, and paid internships for economically disadvantaged students in particular (Beagle & Johnson, 1991), as well as attracting corporate fiscal support for career-relevant curriculum development—which is likely to be a more cost-effective for corporations than investment in extensive new-employee education and workforce development programs (Holton, 1998). Also, college-business partnerships may serve to harness some of the considerable political clout of the business community in support of state budgetary allocations for colleges and universities (Daly, 1992).

Lastly, college-corporate collaboration has the potential for promoting ongoing *alumni* involvement with their alma mater—for example, alumni serving as career mentors for college seniors, or as consultants and advisors to faculty members on the relevance of the college curriculum to career performance expectations.

7. The challenge of institutional *assessment* and *accountability*.

Collaboration among different professionals in the college community is necessary for meaningful and comprehensive institutional assessment because college impact on student learning and development outcomes encompasses multiple student experiences, occurring both inside and outside the classroom. As Banta et al. (1996) emphatically state, "There is, perhaps, no more important principle than this: successful assessment requires collaborative efforts" (p. 35).

Even a cursory review of college catalogues will reveal that the majority of institutional mission statements embrace educational goals that are much broader and diverse than knowledge acquisition. One comprehensive review of research on student outcomes strongly points to the conclusion that college impact hinges on the level of student involvement in both academic and nonacademic activities (Pascarella & Terenzini, 1991). These findings suggest that effective assessment requires cooperation and collaboration across different *organizational units and professional divisions within the college* (Terenzini, 2000).

Moreover, cooperation and collaboration *between different colleges and universities* is necessary for the identification of model practices or "benchmarks"– an essential element of quality assessment and continuous quality improvement. College consortia formed to facilitate inter-institutional data sharing and peer comparisons among institutions of similar size, sector, region, and Carnegie-classification type has already proven to be an indispensable feature of one national instrument designed to assesses the quality of undergraduate education (Kuh, 2001). It has also been observed that some institutions which become involved in benchmarking continue to maintain partnerships with participating institutions after the assessment is completed, or initiate new partnerships with other institutions (Epper, 1999).

Another strong argument for inter-institutional collaboration is the importance of having assessment conducted by "external" or "third-party" evaluators who are not associated with the institution being assessed and have no vested interest in the assessment outcome. Upcraft and Schuh (1996) offer the cogent suggestion that postsecondary institutions form consortia and employ external assessors from institutions other than their own—perhaps as part of an inter-institutional exchange, whereby a member from each institution serves as an external evaluator for the other.

Lastly, inter-institutional coordination and collaboration are critical for accurate assessment of *student persistence to college graduation.* Heretofore, assessment of student retention in higher education has occurred almost exclusively at the level of the individual institution—i.e., assessing the percent of an institution's beginning cohort of students who persist to degree completion at that institution. However, to accurately assess the proportion of students entering the American higher education system who eventually go on to complete a college degree, it is essential to gather cross-institutional data on students who leave their initial institution but transfer, either immediately or eventually, to another institution at which they complete their degree. Thus, inter-institutional data collection is necessary for valid assessment of student retention in the higher education *system*—as opposed to retention at a higher education *institution* (Tinto, 1993). The importance of this distinction is underscored by a large-scale longitudinal study conducted under the auspices of the U.S. Department of Education which revealed that 58% of all baccalaureate degree recipients attended more than one college before completing their degree (Adelman, 1998). This finding suggests that institutional graduation rates will underestimate the overall graduation rate in higher education , and that valid assessment of a very important accountability measure of America's educational system—its national college-graduawtion rate—requires close collaboration among postsecondary institutions to facilitate inter-institutional exchange of student data bases, as well as longitudinal, cross-institutional analysis of student enrollment and re-enrollment patterns.

8. The challenge of maximizing the educational impact of *information technology*.

The recent explosion of information technology now enables interpersonal communication and information dissemination to occur anywhere, anytime, through such technology-mediated mechanisms as electronic mail, online networks, "virtual groups," or "groupware" (Gilbert, 1995). For example, electronic data bases are facilitating worldwide pooling of and access to research findings, and electronic networks now enable scholars to share their thoughts internationally and instantaneously. These technologies have the potential to expand the number and nature of people involved in the collaborative process, and the range of contexts within which collaboration can occur, so that it may take place on campus, off campus, in person, or on line—as well as locally, regionally, nationally, and globally. If information technology is adopted or adapted to foster *interdependent* relationships among its users—above and beyond mere communication or dissemination of information—then it may not only trigger an *information* revolution but a *collaboration* revolution as well.

Conclusion

Less emphasis on individualistic, competitive practices and more emphasis on interdependent, collaborative alliances will help American higher education address its historical mandates for reform and meet its current challenges. Collaborative partnerships have the potential for promoting systemic and enduring change by building mutually productive, interdependent connections *within* the college—among its students, faculty, academic disciplines, and functional divisions, as well as interdependent connections *between* the college and its neighbors—the schools from which its students come, the local community in which its current students reside, and the institutions or organizations to which its future graduates go.

However, for this lofty goal to be realized, explicit encouragement and concrete support from higher educational leaders and central administrators are essential preconditions. Although they may not be directly involved as collaborators in many of the practices cited in the proposed taxonomy, high-level administrators function as key facilitators or promoters of collaboration because they influence the following campus policies and procedures—all of which can affect or determine whether or not collaboration takes place: (a) provision of *incentive systems* that stimulate interest and involvement in collaboration; (b) *resource allocation* in support of collaborative projects; (c) *recruitment and selection* of college personnel with an interest in, or history of collaboration (d) implementation of *orientation* and *development* practices that increase faculty/staff awareness of, and preparation for effective collaboration (e) adoption of *recognition and reward* systems that reinforce collaborative efforts; (f) development of administrative *structures and policies* that reduce boundaries and remove barriers to collaboration across departments, divisions, and administrative units; and (g) creation of institutional vision statements and strategic plans that emphasize the centrality of collaboration to the mission and future direction of the college.

By influencing or implementing the foregoing policies and procedures, college leaders play a pivotal role in creating a campus climate and college culture that is conducive to collaboration among its constituents. In so doing, administrators can also strengthen *campus community*—an institutional goal that over 70% of nationally-surveyed college presidents rate as "very important" for improving the quality of campus life (Carnegie Foundation and American Council on Education, 1989), and which emerged as the most pervasive theme across 120 campus roundtable discussions among 3600 campus leaders (Institute for Research in Higher Education, 1996).

In addition to college administrators, leaders of university systems and state political officials (e.g., governors, legislators) can help create campus conditions that support collaboration within and among colleges or universities under their jurisdiction. They may do so by any of the following means: (a) articulating policies and priorities regarding public expectations of higher education in the state, (b) establishing state information-management systems that can influence inter-institutional communication and data-sharing practices, (c) mandating state accountability measures and institutional-assessment practices, and (d) budgeting and allocating resources based on institutional practices and performance. All of the foregoing policies and procedures can be structured in a fashion that encourages collaboration; for example, institutional performance budgeting could include evidence of collaboration as one criterion in decisions about the total fiscal allocation awarded to colleges and universities. In fact, one study of performance-funded assessment programs has revealed that successful and stable programs are characterized by "collaboration between governors and legislators, state coordinating and university officials, campus leaders and trustees" (Burke, Modarresi, & Serban, 1999, p. 21).

Collaboration among multiple stakeholders in the higher education enterprise, including both those inside and outside the system, can create the foundation needed to approach the futuristic ideal of a "Connected University" or "Transversity"—one which transcends the insular boundaries of the traditional university to encompass transdisciplinary linkages among disciplines, across departments, and between departments and off-campus constituents beyond the campus (Scott & Awbrey, 1993). Such collaborative connections are also likely to encourage interactive, holistic "systems thinking" (Senge, 1994), which has the greatest potential for inducing truly "transformative" change (American Association for Higher Education, 1993) and for producing educational reform that is powerful, pervasive, and persistent.

A Taxonomy of Collaborative Practices in Higher Education

Introduction

All practices cited in the following taxonomy clearly involve interpersonal *interaction*; however, when this interaction is also characterized by *interdependence*, i.e., when the parties involved share common goals, engage in coordinated effort, and experience mutual benefits, then nature of the interactive relationship is elevated to a higher level which may be accurately labeled *collaboration*. This capacity or potential for interdependence was used as a guiding criterion to identify and select practices for inclusion in the taxonomy.

The proposed classification system embraces more than 150 practices that are clustered into seven broad categories. Within these broad categories, specific practices are identified and organized into subcategories. Each general category of collaboration is accompanied by a research-based rationale highlighting its contemporary significance for higher education.

1. COLLABORATION BETWEEN *STUDENTS*

Recent evidence supporting the educational impact of student collaboration is provided by a meta-analysis of its effects on college students' academic performance in science, math, engineering and technology conducted by the National Institute for Science Education. (Meta-analysis may be defined as a quantitative synthesis of many studies relating to a particular educational variable or instructional method.) Over 500 studies of small-group collaboration were included in this meta-analysis, and it was found that collaborative learning had a "robust" positive effect on such educational outcomes as (a) academic achievement, (b) student retention, and (c) attitude (liking) of the subject matter (Cooper, 1997).

Additional evidence underscoring the effectiveness of student collaboration for promoting students' academic achievement is provided by collegiate research on peer teaching/learning which indicates that both the peer learner and the peer teacher (peer tutor) learn significantly from such collaborative experiences (Whitman, 1988). For example, college students display deeper levels of understanding for concepts they teach to other students (Bargh & Schul, 1980; Benware & Deci, 1984), and they achieve greater mastery of course content (Johnson, Sulzer-Azaroff, & Mass, 1977). McKeachie, et al., concluded from their review of higher education research on teaching and learning that, "the best answer to the question of what is the most effective method of teaching is that it depends on the goal, the student, the content and the teachers. But the next best answer is students teaching other students" (1986, p. 63).

Fostering collaboration among students also represents an effective instructional strategy for promoting student retention. Collaboration among students fosters their social in-

---

tegration into the college community—an experience that is strongly associated with student retention (Tinto, 1993). The importance of collaborative study groups for the retention and achievement of *underrepresented* students, in particular, is supported by the work of Uri Treisman (Treisman, 1985; Green, 1989). Treisman studied the effect of collaborative learning on African-American students who entered the University of California-Berkeley as math or science majors. Five-year retention rates at Berkeley for African-American students who participated in collaborative learning workshops was 65%, while the retention rate for black non-participants was 41%.

These findings have been replicated in a 5-year longitudinal study of underrepresented Latino students enrolled in mathematics, science or engineering programs at California Polytechnic State University, Pomona. This study revealed that fewer than 4% of the Latino students who participated in out-of-class collaborative learning sessions withdrew or were academically dismissed, compared to 40% of non-participants (Bonsangue, 1993).

Lastly, promoting collaboration among students while they are in college serves to cultivate interpersonal relations that are critical for success in life after college (Cross, 1985). Arthur Chickering eloquently expresses the need for higher education to more intentionally develop students' ability to collaborate and promote their capacity for interdependence: "To the extent that we emphasize isolated, individual, competitive work and products, we both mislead students about the nature of work and construct obstacles to their interpersonal development. It is in the area of *interdependence* of all work that higher education has a largely uncharted world to explore. And in such exploration we will also find ways to help our students move toward increased capacity for intimacy" (1969, p. 210).

The collaborative practices identified in this section of the taxonomy illustrate how student collaboration can be in-

---

tentionally fostered outside the classroom and across the curriculum.

• MAJOR FORMS OF COLLABORATION BETWEEN *STUDENTS*

1.1 *Small Group Discussion* (a.k.a., "Buzz Groups"): several students join together *during class* to express their views and hear the views of their peers with respect to some course issue.

1.2 *Group Project/Group Report*: a group of students collaborate on an assigned project which they typically research and discuss *outside of class*. The group's work product is presented in the form of a written report (e.g., term paper), oral report (e.g., panel presentation), or some combination thereof. Grades are assigned on an individual or group basis, or some combination thereof. (For example, the performance of both the individual and the group may be graded and then averaged to generate each student's grade for the project).

1.3 *Study Groups*: Students meet in *small groups outside of class* to help each other study and master course material. Traditionally, the term "study group" has been used to refer to a group of students who come together to study for an upcoming exam; however, out-of-class student groups may also be formed to accomplish other academic tasks. Listed below is a more comprehensive list of additional study-group tasks and functions.
• *Note-Taking* Groups: students convene immediately after class has ended to compare and share notes.

- *Reading* Groups: students collaborate after completing reading assignments to compare their highlighting and margin notes.

- *Library Research* Groups: students join together to conduct library research and combat "library anxiety."

- *Test-Results Review* Groups: After receiving test results, students review their individual tests together to help members identify sources of their mistakes and view "model" answers that received maximum credit.

- *Group Conferences with the Instructor*: Students visit the course instructor, as a group, during office hours to seek additional assistance in preparing for exams or completing assignments.

1.4 ***Collaborative* Learning**: small-group learning experience in which group members reach *consensus* with respect to some decision or action.

Scholars in the fields of English and Literature have argued that *consensus* must be reached by group discussants in order to ensure that collaboration has occurred, and they refer to such consensus-reaching, small-group work as "collaborative learning" (e.g., Bruffee, 1981; Wiener, 1986). Historically, this consensus-focused definition of collaborative learning has its roots in the professional education of medical students who collaborated in small groups to reach unified diagnostic decisions—which often proved superior to decisions reached individually (Abercrombie (1960).

1.5 ***Cooperative* Learning**: a learner-centered instructional process typically characterized by the following distinctive features: (a) small, *intentionally formed* groups, (b)

---

well-defined *roles* for all group members, (c) group members work *interdependently* on the same learning task to produce a *common or unified product*, (d) group members are held *individually accountable* for their personal performance, and (e) instructor's role is that of *facilitator* of or *consultant* to the learning groups.

Arguably, cooperative learning is the most operationally well-defined and procedurally structured form of collaboration among students. Its roots lie in the educational philosophy of John Dewey and the social psychology of Kurt Lewin, while its evolution into a systematic instructional procedure probably originated in the work of David and Robert Johnson and Robert Slavin in the early 1960s. At the precollege level, cooperative learning (defined in terms of the aforementioned distinctive features) has been the most researched and empirically well-documented form of student collaboration, demonstrating robust positive effects on multiple student outcomes (Johnson et al., 1981). The realization of these positive outcomes appears to vary commensurately with the number of its critical features that are carefully implemented (Slavin, 1990).

Since its initial conception, a large number of procedural variations or cooperative learning "structures" have been created. Listed below is a sample of some of the major types of cooperative learning structures. For a comprehensive enumeration and detailed description of a large variety of cooperative learning structures, see Kagan (1992), Millis & Cottell (1998), and Cuseo (2002).

Major Cooperative-Learning *Structures:*

• *Paining* Structures: *Dyadic* (*Two*-Member) Teams
Example: "Cooperative Note-Taking Pairs"—at a designated point *during* a lecture, students pair up and *ask each other questions* such as: "What have you got in your notes thus far?" or, "What are the most important points that have been presented?" Each member of the pair must take something from the other's notes to include in his own. (Johnson, Johnson, & Smith, 1991)

• *Small-Group* Structures: 3-4 Member Teams
Example: "Team Statement"—all team members first construct *individual position statements* about a topic or issue, then teammates join together and attempt to *integrate* their separate sentences into *one unified* statement (paragraph) which attempts to capture the essence of the team's collective thought. (Kagan, 1992)

• Structures Explicitly Designed To Promote *Positive Interdependence*
Example: "Jigsaw"—teams are assigned a general topic and each teammate assumes responsibility for becoming an "expert" on one subtopic or *piece* of this general topic. Then members leave their teams to join members of other teams who are also "experts" on the same subtopic. After meeting in different expert groups, students return to their home team and teach their area of expertise to their teammates. The final outcome of this process is the *piecing together* of separate subtopics (like a "jigsaw" puzzle), resulting in a more comprehensive understanding of the whole topic. (Aronson, et al., 1978)

- Structures Explicitly Designed To Promote *Individual Accountability*

Example: "Roundtable"—teams are provided with a *single pen and a single piece of paper* (or transparency). One teammate records a contribution on the paper and then passes the paper and pen on to another teammate who does the same. The paper and pen are progressively passed *around the table* until all team members have recorded an idea, thus ensuring individual accountability for each member. (Kagan, 1992)

- Structures Designed To Facilitate *Team Formation*

Example: "Corners"—students *move to one corner* of the room based on a personal *choice, preference, or characteristic*. The instructor then forms smaller groups or teams of students, either from within the corner of the room they occupy—creating homogeneous teams, or by mixing students from different corners of the room—creating heterogeneous teams. (Kagan, 1992)

- Structures Designed To Promote *Between-Team Interaction* and *Whole-Class Synergy*

Example: "Carousel Feedback"—teams *rotate* around the room to view the completed *products of other teams* (e.g., charts, posters, concept maps, artistic depictions), and record their *reactions or comments on a feedback sheet* that is posted by the products. Teams then return to their own product to *incorporate* any *new ideas* acquired during the tour (Kagan, 1998).

1.6 *Problem-Based Learning (PBL)*

An inquiry-based method of learning whereby students work in small groups to inductively solve complex, real-world problems (e.g., case studies). Groups first identify and research concepts or principles they need to know to progress through the problem. As they work on the problem, the instructor encourages them to further define what they know and do not know. Group members then discuss what resources are needed to research unanswered questions, where these resources may be located, and who will be responsible for acquiring the needed information. After completing their research, teammates integrate their acquired knowledge and apply it to solve the problem at hand (Duch, Allen, & White, 2000; Engel, 1991).

1.7 *Guided Design*

A systematic strategy for developing students' decision-making skills with respect to course concepts in which learners work in 5-6 member teams. Students are first asked to identify the problem embedded in a situation described by the instructor. After teams agree on the problem and an approach to solving it, they compare their work with a printed "feedback" page which shows how other teams have responded; students are then asked to reflect on and consider alternative solution strategies developed by others.

Teamwork on a "guided design" problem may take from 2-15 hours, and students are expected to learn problem-relevant subject matter outside of class time. (See Wales & Sager [1977] for more detail information about this collaborative approach, including sample material for guided-design projects and related books, articles, and dissertations.)

1.8 *Learning Communities*

The origin of learning communities dates back to the innovative work of Meiklejohn (1932) at the University of Wisconsin. Since 1985, The Washington Center for the Improvement of the Quality of Undergraduate Education has served as a national clearinghouse for the development and dissemination of learning community models.

The defining or distinguishing feature of learning communities—i.e., what all types or models of learning commu-

---

nities have in common—is that a cohort of students co-register for and enroll in a block of two or more courses together during the same academic term. While this is the common theme that unites all learning-community models, variations on this theme can occur with respect to: (a) the number of courses students take together during the term—which may range from two to an entire course load (4-5 courses); (b) whether the cohort comprises the entire class, a subset of a larger class, or some combination thereof (e.g., a cohort may comprise the entire enrollment of a small English composition class and co-enroll in a history course with a larger class size); and (c) the degree of instructional coordination among faculty teaching courses containing the student cohort (e.g., no coordination by instructors whatsoever, some instructional coordination of course content and assignments, or full coordination in which all instructors team-teach all courses together as part of an integrated, interdisciplinary program).

For classification purposes, learning communities may best be viewed as an umbrella program, embracing a variety of different curricular structures within which are nested two major forms of collaboration: (a) collaboration between students, and (b) collaboration between faculty. Those components of learning community models that primarily involve the first form of collaboration (student-student collaboration) will be discussed within this category of the taxonomy. (Components of learning community models that showcase collaboration between faculty will be discussed later—under the category of faculty-faculty collaboration.)

Listed below are six basic learning-community models. These prototypes may be modified to produce multiple permutations or hybrid models. For a more comprehensive overview of diverse learning community models and specific strategies for their implementation, see Gabelnick, MacGregor, Matthews, & Smith (1990), and Shapiro & Levine (1999).

Basic *Models (Types)* of Learning Communities

• *Course Linking (a.k.a., Paired or Linked Courses)*: a cohort of students co-register for the same *pair* of courses which they take concurrently during the same academic term. One common way that paired courses are linked is in terms of some shared course content which relates to a broader topic, with each course developing a different aspect of this cross-cutting topic. (For example, a biology and psychology course may each address different aspects of the relationship between brain and mind.) Another common way in which courses are linked is by pairing a small skill-building, process-oriented course (e.g., English composition, Speech, or Freshman Seminar) with a larger, content-focused, lecture-driven course (e.g., an introductory general education course). Students then apply the skills they are learning in their smaller process-oriented course to the content covered in the larger lecture course.

Course linking may be adapted and extended to form two-term sequential learning communities whereby two to three courses are linked each term, so the majority of students stay in the same learning communities throughout the entire academic year (e.g., their critical freshman year).

• *Learning Clusters*: a group of students co-register for the same cluster of *3-4 courses* during a given semester. Clustered courses comprise a substantial portion, or the entire load, of a student's semester schedule. Faculty teaching courses in a cluster may or may not integrate their course content; however, in "integrated clusters," a one-hour weekly seminar taught jointly by the various faculty whose courses comprise the cluster, serves to integrate ideas and identify cross-cutting themes.

Clusters may also be tailored to meet the special needs of student subpopulations. For instance, to accommodate the off-campus responsibilities of working commuter students, clustered courses may be scheduled back to back so that students can make most effective use of their limited time on campus. Or, honors students may take a thematic learning cluster in which two of their clustered courses are limited only to honor students, while the remaining course is a larger lecture class that is open to all students. Thus, a sense of community can develop among honor students without segregating them entirely and negating their potentially positive influence on other (non-honors) students.

- *Freshman Interest Groups (FIGs):* a special type of learning cluster whereby small cohorts of freshmen (20-30 students) are recruited via summer mailing and new-student orientation to register for the *same 3-4 courses*—which often represent a related set of general education requirements or pre-major courses in the students' field of academic interest. This cohort of freshmen travel together as a *subset* of about 20-30 students to three or four larger classes which they all have in common. One of these courses typically has a small-class component that involves only FIG students (e.g., a lab session or discussion group formed from a course that has a larger number of students).

A trained upper-division student is assigned as a *peer advisor* to each FIG, and meets with these freshmen regularly throughout the term (e.g. in a weekly proseminar), as well as with the coordinator of the entire FIG program—a staff member or graduate teaching assistant. Peer advisors are selected on the basis of their prior record of academic performance or student leadership and are brought together for an extended orientation and training session before the start of the academic year. The peer advisors receive academic credit for leading the FIG group, typically as an independent study or internship in leadership development.

Faculty teaching in the FIG may attend meetings be-

---

tween students and their peer advisor, or other faculty may be invited to the meeting as guest speakers, serving to promote faculty-student contact outside the classroom.

• *Interest Groups in the Major* (a.k.a., *Junior Interest Groups*): upper-division students (typically juniors) co-register for the same *three required courses in their major*, and a *graduate teaching assistant* in the same academic discipline convenes *weekly meetings* to assist the undergraduates in these three courses.

• *Federated Learning Communities (FLCs)*: a small cohort of students register for the same three courses which are offered under the rubric of an *overarching theme* and which often includes an additional 3-unit discussion seminar. This seminar is designed to integrate the material taught in the three separate courses and is led by a *master learner*—a faculty member whose educational background is not in any of the academic disciplines being taught—who takes the three courses along with the cohort of students.

At some institutions, the federated learning community is provided with an office, lounge, or seminar room in order to provide a "home" to foster informal interaction and a sense of belongingness among FLC members.

• *Coordinated Studies Programs*: a group of 20-25 students takes *all* their courses together in a given semester. The 4-5 courses are organized under an overarching theme and are co-designed and *team-taught* by the same group of faculty. The classes are usually scheduled in *longer time blocks* to allow for alternative learning experiences, such as extended discussions or field trips. Typically, the program offerings and faculty teams are changed each term; faculty members teach exclusively within one coordinated study program per term, and students register for only one coordinated studies program as their entire course load for that term.

1.9 *Cluster Colleges* (a.k.a., *Colleges-Within-A-College* Program): At large colleges or universities, students who have similar academic interests (e.g., humanities majors) do their learning in a circumscribed area or subunit of the campus—i.e., they take courses in the same, proximally located buildings, and if they are residential students, they live in the same or nearby units.

The primary objective of cluster colleges is to reduce the "impersonal" nature of the large university experience and stimulate discourse among learners within the same college who share the same physical space and similar academic interests.

1.10 *Peer Teaching/Learning* Programs: students who are more advanced in their understanding of subject matter or in their development of an academic skill, are enlisted to provide learning assistance to less advanced students.

Major *Types* of Peer Teaching/Learning Arrangements:

• *Peer Tutoring*: one-on-one or group assistance provided to students by specially trained peers, typically orchestrated under the aegis of the Learning Assistance Center or Learning Resource Center.

• *Supplemental Instruction (SI)*: a student who has done exceptionally well in a course re-attends the same class along with novice learners, helping them individually and in group sessions that are regularly scheduled outside of class time. These supplemental out-of-class sessions often carry one additional unit of college credit. Typically, "high-risk," or "killer" courses that have high dropout or failure rates are targeted for this peer teaching/learning strategy. (Note: Supple-

mental instruction is occasionally, though less commonly, referred to as an "Adjunct Instructional Program [AIP])."

• *Writing Fellows*: upper-division students with strong
writing skills receive extensive peer-teaching training and are
deployed to an undergraduate class (particularly large introductory courses in their major) where they read and respond
to the papers of all students.

• *PBL Facilitators*: upper-class undergraduates who
have completed a course taught via problem-based learning
(PBL) serve as roving facilitators for lower-division students
taking the same course.

1.10 **Peer Mentors**: more experienced students (e.g.,
juniors or seniors) serve as advisors or mentors to less-experienced students (e.g., freshmen or sophomores) for the primary purpose of promoting the academic success of the less-
experienced students and for the secondary purpose of promoting the development of the more experienced students
(e.g., leadership development).

1.11 **Peer Academic Advisors**: experienced students are
trained to serve as advising facilitators for less-experienced
students, helping them prepare for meetings with their faculty advisors and assisting them with the mechanics of advising (e.g., dealing with the course-registration process).

1.12 **Group Advising**: students with similar academic
or pre-professional interests are advised as a group (e.g., advising sessions for a group of sociology majors), one objective of which is to promote peer collaboration and mutual
support with respect to academic and career planning.

1.13 **Peer Resident Advisors**: more experienced students

living in a college residence provide advice and support to less-experienced students living in the same residence.

1.14 *Peer Counselors*: students trained in counseling techniques serve as paraprofessional counselors for students who seek their assistance on personal matters (e.g., social and emotional issues).

1.15 *Alumni Mentors*: an undergraduate student and a college alumnus are paired so that the alumnus may share career information and work experience with the student, or model career-related skills.

2. COLLABORATION BETWEEN *FACULTY*

Scholars calling for curricular reform have argued that the exponential growth in knowledge has fractionated college faculty into atomized, isolated academic subfields which impede both intra-disciplinary and interdisciplinary collaboration (Association of American Colleges, 1988; Walter, 1988). The term "invisible college" has been coined to capture the fact that subgroups of faculty specialists, with narrowly defined scholarly interests, have more in common with subdisciplinary specialists in the same field who are housed at other universities than they do with fellow faculty on their home campus (McCloskey, 1991). Such hyperspecialization leads Tompkins (1992) to conclude that, "Nobody has to talk to anybody because none of what we do *depends* on anyone else" (p. 15).

It has been said that this growing lack of professional interdependence is contributing to the development of a faculty culture of "lone rangers" with "frontier values" in which individual productivity is valued at the expense of academic collaboration and integration (Ewell, 1994, p. 27). Such rugged individualism works against the development of meaningful interdisciplinary connections among courses that could create a more coherent college curriculum, and it discourages the type interdisciplinary research that is most likely to result in comprehensive and innovative solutions to real-world problems—which almost invariably are interdisciplinary in nature. As Edwards (1999) states emphatically, "This observation appears unexceptionable: in so many cases, the most provocative and interesting work is done at the intersections where disciplines meet, or by collaborators blending seemingly disparate disciplines to attack real problems afresh. Whether this work be labeled cross-disciplinary, interdisciplinary, or multidisciplinary, it fits awkwardly with the university's traditionally defined disciplinary boundaries" (p. 19).

Furthermore, a body of quantitative and qualitative research indicates that faculty who engage in collaborative scholarship tend to be more prolific, proficient, and innovative than faculty who work alone (Austin & Baldwin, 1991; Finklestein, 1984). In addition, collaborative researchers also report higher levels of cognitive risk-taking, work satisfaction, and overall psychological well-being (Austin & Baldwin, 1991). Similar benefits have been reported by faculty who engage in interdisciplinary team-teaching ventures (Buckley, 1999; Davis, 1995).

The practices listed in this section of the taxonomy illustrate how collaboration among faculty can be used to enrich the processes of teaching and research, integrate knowledge within and between disciplines, and promote faculty development.

• MAJOR FORMS OF COLLABORATION BETWEEN *FACULTY*

2.1 *Team-Teaching* **Programs**: two or more faculty combine to design or teach a course.

Types of Team-Teaching Arrangements:

• *Star* Team (a.k.a., *Master-Teacher* Pattern): one faculty member is primarily responsible for planning and conducting the course, but faculty experts are invited to class to address course topics that relate to their particular areas of expertise.

• *Specialist* Team: two or more faculty members collaborate to design a course, but teaching duties are divided according to the faculty members' area of expertise.

• *Interdisciplinary* Team: faculty from different academic disciplines collaborate to design and/or instruct a course which is intended to integrate two or more disciplines.

2.2 *Learning Community* **Models**
In the course linking and learning clusters models (previously described under the rubric of student-student collaboration), instructors teaching in the "linked" or "clustered" courses typically collaborate to coordinate their syllabi and assignments for the cohort of students who are enrolled in their linked or clustered courses. In the "coordinated studies program," all instructors involved in the program collaborate to team-teach each course together.

Also, in many learning community models, faculty will

(a) come together for pre-semester, course-planning retreats; (b) audit each other's courses before team-teaching together; and/or (c) meet together for weekly seminars during the semester in which they are team-teaching.

2.3 *Faculty Research/Scholarship Teams* (a.k.a., "Collaborative Scholarship"): two or more faculty members combine to coordinate their efforts in pursuit of a common research/scholarship goal, with the faculty collaborators sharing responsibility and credit for the final product. If the faculty members are from different academic disciplines, the term "interdisciplinary" research/scholarship would apply.

2.4 *Veteran Faculty-New Faculty Mentoring* **Program**: an experienced faculty member serves as a mentor for an inexperienced or newly hired faculty member to help the latter (protegee) to successfully meet her professional responsibilities and promote her professional development.

2.5 *Partners in Learning (nee, Master Faculty* **Program***):* a "buddy system" in which faculty work in pairs, with one member serving as a regular observer in a colleague's course, visiting once a week during the academic term. Both faculty members regularly interview several students to discuss the students' thoughts about the course, the teaching/ learning process, their personal concerns, and any other matters relating to the course. Besides regular class observations and student interviews, a third component of this collaborative model consists of regularly scheduled conversations between the two faculty members and, once a month, all faculty pairs on campus convene to discuss their experiences. Typically, the faculty members reverse roles the following semester, with the observed faculty member becoming the observer and vice versa.

2.6 *Mutual Mentoring Caucuses*: A group of 4-5 faculty agree to work together on issues of improving or documenting teaching effectiveness by visiting one another's classes, reviewing each other's teaching materials, and interviewing each other's students.

2.7 *Collaborative Academic Departments*: departmental faculty function as a team in which individual members have complementary roles and responsibilities based on their specific areas of expertise or special talents. The department works to blend its members' different specializations into a unified whole, and faculty are rewarded not only for individual achievements, but also for their collective, departmental achievement (e.g., departmental teaching effectiveness and research productivity).

2.8 *Collaboratories*: infrastructures of computer hardware, software, and related technological resources designed to create an electronic, cross-disciplinary community of scientists and engineers who engage in distal, asynchronous collaboration on research projects and share each other's research findings.

3. FACULTY-STUDENT COLLABORATION

Postsecondary research has consistently demonstrated that college students' success is strongly influenced by the quality and quantity of student-faculty interaction *outside* the classroom. Such contact has been found to correlate positively with students' (a) satisfaction with the college experience (Astin, 1977) (b) retention (Tinto, 1993), (c) academic

---

achievement (Astin, 1993), (d) personal and intellectual development (Endo & Harpel, 1982), (e) critical thinking (Wilson 1975), and (f) educational aspirations—such as decisions to pursue advanced (graduate) education (Stoecker, Pascarella, & Wolfle, 1988). Similar positive correlations between frequency of student-faculty contact and cognitive growth have been reported for first-year *transfer* students (Volkwein, King, & Terenzini, 1986).

Despite these well-documented positive outcomes, the *frequency* of faculty-student contact outside the classroom is *decreasing* in higher education because faculty are spending more of their non-teaching time on endeavors relating to research and publication, leaving the brunt of out-of-class contact with undergraduates to student affairs' staff (Kuh, Schuh, Whitt, & Associates, 1991).

The practices cited in this section of the taxonomy illustrate how faculty-student contact outside the classroom can be intentionally increased in a wide variety of collaborative contexts and relationships, which include: mentoring, tutoring, teaching, research, and residential life.

• MAJOR FORMS OF *FACULTY-STUDENT* COLLABORATION

3.1 *Faculty-Student Mentoring* Programs: a faculty member serves as mentor to facilitate an undergraduate student's academic success. (For example, a minority faculty member serves as a mentor for a minority undergraduate).

3.2 *Faculty-In-Residence* Program: a teaching faculty member lives in a student residence and provides out-of-class instruction, advising, or mentoring assistance to residential students who co-occupy the same unit.

3.3 *Faculty-Student Research Teams*: a faculty member involves undergraduate students in her field of research, for which the students gain experience as research assistants and a potential product for use as a senior honors thesis or professional publication.

3.4 *Undergraduate Fellows* **Program**: undergraduate student fellows receive stipends for working 10-20 hours per week with faculty mentors on collaborative research projects or creative productions.

3.5 *Faculty-Student Teaching Teams*: a faculty member co-teaches a course with an experienced undergraduate. (For example, a faculty member and a college senior team-teach a freshman seminar.)

3.6 *Undergraduate Teaching Assistant Programs (UTAPs)*: Upper-division students work closely with faculty mentors to gain insight into the teaching role, and obtain first-hand teaching experience. Students receive academic credit for their work as undergraduate teaching assistants and for their participation in a preparatory seminar covering course planning, classroom instruction, and student evaluation.

3.7 *Student Management Teams (SMTs)*: a team of 4-6 students is selected by their instructor to assume responsibility for ensuring quality teaching by serving as "student managers" for a course. The role of this student management team is to solicit comments from other students and dialogue with the instructor about possible course improvements. Student managers sometimes participate in a training program to prepare them for this role.

3.8 *Small Group Instructional Diagnosis (SGID)*, a.k.a., *Small Group Intructional Feedback (SGIF):* small groups of students (4-6 members) from a class participate in structured interviews during the term which are conducted by an outside facilitator (typically a faculty peer or faculty development specialist), in the absence of the course instructor, for the purpose of making course improvements. Students discuss the course in these small groups and attempt to reach consensus on two key questions: (a) What helps you learn in this course? and (b) What improvements would you like and how would you suggest they be made? The outside facilitator records the students' ideas on the board and attempts to clarify and organize them into a coherent series of recommendations for the instructor.

3.9 *Collaborative Course Development*: faculty members designing new interdisciplinary courses, often relating to contemporary issues or emerging areas interest, draw on a panel that includes students and alumni to assist in course planning and syllabus development.

3.10 *Faculty-Student Support Service Teams (FSSTs)*: Student assistants help other students, staff members, and faculty in the area of information technology, capitalizing on their familiarity and experience with computers to help combat support-service shortages on campus. In the process, students acquire technical and human service skills that prepare them for higher-paying, part-time work in information industries while they are still in college, and for entry-level technology positions after college.

3.11 *ESL-Linked Transitional Courses*: English as a Second Language (ESL) instructor participates as a learner in an academic discipline-based course (e.g., History) which contains a portion of ESL students, and helps these students master the course material.
3.12 *Federated Learning Communities (FLC):* a learn-

ing community model whereby faculty-student collaboration occurs when the faculty member takes the same courses as the cohort of students, and serves as a "master learner" to help students master and integrate concepts taught in the different courses.

4. CROSS-FUNCTIONAL TEAMS

(Collaboration Between Members of Different Functional Units or Professional Divisions Within the College)

Students' academic success and personal development depend not only on the quality of the curriculum and classroom instruction, but also on the effectiveness of two other major divisions or educational units of the college: Student Development Services (a.k.a., Student Affairs) and Academic Support Services. When instructional faculty interface and collaborate with these two key student-service divisions, combinatorial or synergistic effects are likely to be exerted on student learning and development, thereby maximizing the impact and quality of the college experience.

Student development professionals have long been aware of the fact that the success of a college's student development program is contingent upon collaborative relations between student affairs staff and faculty (American College Personnel Association, 1975). In a seminal and highly influential text outlining future directions for the profession of student affairs, Miller & Prince (1976) categorically conclude that, "an institution's commitment to student development is directly proportional to the number of collaborative links between the student affairs staff and the faculty" (p. 155). More recently, the Joint Task Force on Student Learning—a collaborative initiative created by the American Association for

Higher Education (AAHE), the American College Personnel Association (ACPA), and the National Association of Student Personnel Administrators (NASPA)—has been created to promote approaches to student learning that reflect connection or integration between educational experiences occurring inside and outside the classroom. As two members of the joint task force argue, "It takes a whole college to educate a whole student. Administrative leaders can rethink the conventional organization of colleges and universities to create more inventive structures and processes that integrate academic and student affairs; [and] offer professional-development opportunities for people to cooperate across institutional boundaries" (Engelkemeyer & Brown, 1988, p.12).

Collaborative practices cited within this section of the taxonomy (subsection 4.1) illustrate how the divisions of Academic and Student Affairs can collaborate to connect learning in courses with learning on campus—by means of integrative assignments, guest speakers, living-learning communities, and jointly planned programs—such as orientation and graduation.

A second important cross-functional intersection in higher education is that which occurs between classroom instruction conducted by college faculty and academic-support services provided by learning assistance professionals. The need for and potential value of collaboration between these two academic units is highlighted by national survey research which indicates that "fear of academic failure" and "help with academic skills" are among the most frequently cited concerns of beginning college students (Astin & Associates, 1996). Research also suggests that students who earn good grades during their first term are far more likely to continue in college and graduate than are first-term students who do not experience initial academic success (Pantages & Creedan, 1978). Furthermore, decisions to stay or leave college have been found to correlate more strongly with first-year students' academic achievement than with their pre-enrollment characteristics (Pascarella & Chapman, 1983).

Additional research demonstrates that (a) students generally *under-utilize* academic support services (Friedlander, 1980), particularly those students who are in most need of support (Knapp & Karabenick, 1988), and (b) students who do seek and receive academic assistance improve their *academic performance* and experience increased *academic self-efficacy*—i.e., heightened sense of self-perceived control of, and higher self-expectations for, future academic success (Smith, Walter, & Hoey, 1992).

Taken together, this collection of findings strongly suggest that first-year students who receive learning assistance from academic support services during the first year of college are more likely to be retained and achieve higher levels of academic performance. Included in this section of the taxonomy (subsection 4.2) are collaborative practices involving partnerships between classroom faculty and two key academic-support services: (a) the college library, and (b) the college learning-resource center.

Lastly, this section of the taxonomy includes illustrations of cross-functional teams whose collaboration occurs in the form of all-college committees and task forces (subsection 4.3).

• KEY TYPES OF *CROSS-FUNCTIONAL* TEAMS

4.1 Educational Partnerships between the Divisions of *Academic Affairs & Student Life*

• Student development professionals help faculty coordinate their *course assignments* with *on-campus events* to better integrate the curriculum and co-curriculum.

• Offices of Academic and Student Affairs jointly plan and orchestrate *student transition experiences* (e.g., new-student orientation and college graduation).

• Faculty members and student development professionals *team-teach* a course (e.g., freshman seminar, senior seminar, or leadership development course).

• Instructors in *freshman orientation seminars* and *senior capstone seminars* construct *course assignments* that require students to connect with and utilize student development services (e.g., meet with advising or career development professionals to map out a long-term academic or professional development plan).

• *Critical-moment* learning teams comprised of members from Student Life and Academic Affairs respond jointly and immediately to provide an ad hoc educational program designed to help students cope with, or learn from, a just-experienced campus incident or trauma—such as a student suicide or accidental death. (This practice can be expanded to include regional, national, or international incidents.)

• *Career development professionals* collaborate with *departmental faculty* members to help students majoring in their academic discipline develop career plans that are relevant to the students' academic major.

• *Living-Learning Communities/Centers*: residence-based programming involving collaboration between academic and residential-life professionals to provide combined academic and student development programming. For example, faculty may teach, hold office hours, or live in the student residence. The living-learning community may also include a "guest in residence"—such as an artist, social and political activist, or visiting academic scholar.

At large institutions, living-learning communities are typically designed to provide students with a small-college atmosphere. At small colleges, they are often built around some educational theme (e.g., different "theme houses" focusing on different issues, such as diversity, wellness, or internationalism).

4.2 Educational Partnerships between *Classroom Instructors* and *Academic Support Services*

• *Faculty-Librarian* partnerships designed to provide *course-integrated library instruction* whereby *information literacy* (information search-and-retrieval skill development) is integrated with course content. For example, librarians and professors team-teach or co-design courses, components of courses, or out-of-class assignments that integrate library-research skills with course content.

• *Faculty* provide information about their courses to *learning assistance professionals* in order to enhance the relevance and effectiveness of academic support and tutorial services. (For example, instructors provide sample reading assignments or lecture videotapes for tutorial use in the college Learning Center).

• Course instructors collaborate with learning assistance professionals to execute an effective *referral system* for students experiencing *academic difficulty* in their courses.

• *Early-alert (early-warning) systems*: course instructors alert academic advisors or learning assistance professionals about students in their classes who are in academic jeopardy *at or before midterm* by means of a *formal feedback system* (e.g., "midterm progress reports").

• *Supplemental Instruction (SI)*: a learning assistance professional attends a "high-risk course" and conducts regularly scheduled, supplemental tutorial sessions outside of class time.

• Instructors *in freshman seminars* or *student success courses* devise class *assignments* that connect students with learning assistance professionals (e.g., to complete self-assessment inventories on learning styles or learning habits).

4.3 **Cross-functional** *committees, task forces, and conference teams* **focusing on issues of** *college-wide concern.*

• All-college *enrollment management* committees comprised of college admissions representatives and college personnel concerned with student retention.

• *Assessment* task forces involving a cross-section of institutional researchers, faculty, and student development professionals.

• Cross-functional teams of college administrators, support staff, and faculty designed to promote *total quality management (TQM)* or *continuous quality improvement (CQI).*

• *Conference teams* comprised of faculty and administrators travel to and attend the same professional conference focused on a theme of mutual interest (e.g., assessment or student success)—with the intention of collaborating upon return to their home campus to implement conference-acquired information in a comprehensive and coordinated fashion. (Note: Some conference organizers offer reduced individual registration-fee rates for faculty and administrators who come as a team of conferees from the same campus.)

5. *INTER-INSTITUTIONAL* COLLABORATION

(Collaboration Between Different Undergraduate Institutions)

Collaboration between different colleges and universities has been used as a vehicle for reaching a variety of institutional goals which include: (a) expanding the curriculum—e.g., via cross-registration agreements, (b) reducing institutional costs—e.g., pooling resources to share the travel costs and services of a guest speaker or consultant, (c) promoting campus diversity—e.g., via student or faculty exchanges, (d) promoting students' educational advancement—e.g., collaboration between 2- to 4-year colleges to stimulate successful transfer, and (e) facilitating institutional assessment and self-improvement—e.g., benchmarking.

Alexander Astin (1991) argues that inter-institutional collaboration could be expanded further to develop "cooperative systems" of performance-based assessment and funding in which, "Monetary incentives are based on the aggregate performance of an entire system. Under such a cooperative model, institutions would have maximum incentive to facilitate each other's performance, since the success of any one brings in resources that are shared by all the others" (p. 228). For example, two- and four-year institutions in a state system could collaborate and be rewarded for collaborative initiatives that result in increased transfer rates.

In contemporary higher education, collaboration between 2- and 4-year colleges to promote transfer is a particularly compelling form of inter-institutional collaboration for several reasons. (1) The *total number* of potential two- to four-year college transfer students in American higher education is *sizable and growing*. More than 50% of all first-year col-

---

lege students attend two-year institutions (California Community Colleges, 1994; Parnell, 1986), and student enrollment at 2-year institutions is increasing at a faster rate than it is at 4-year colleges and universities (National Center for Educational Statistics, 1993). Simply stated, more 2-year college students will have the potential for making the transition to 4-year institutions than at any other time in our nation's history (Giles-Gee, 1994).

(2) Workplace projections indicate that the *majority of all new jobs* in this country during the 21st century will require some type of *baccalaureate preparation* (Arciniega, 1990; Johnson & Packard, 1987). Students who transfer from two- to four-year institutions to complete a baccalaureate degree have been found to achieve comparable career benefits as students who start and finish at four-year colleges; for example, it has been found that they earn comparable salaries and report similar levels of job satisfaction (Pascarella, 1997; Pascarella & Terenzini, 1991).

(3) There is a significant *gap* between the number of students who enter 2-year colleges with the *intention* of transferring to 4-year institutions and the number who *actually* do. Students who begin higher education at 2-year colleges with the intention of achieving a baccalaureate degree will receive, on average, 15% fewer B.A. degrees than those who enter higher education at 4-year institutions, even when controlling for students' socioeconomic background, academic ability, high school achievement, and educational aspirations at college entry (Astin, 1975, 1977, 1993; Pascarella & Terenzini, 1991). Nationally, since the 1970s, the number of students transferring from 2-year to 4-year colleges has *decreased* relative to the total community-college enrollment (California Community Colleges, 1994), despite the fact that 57% of community college students earn at least 60 semester hours of college credit and 75% earn four or more semester hours of credit during their 2-year college experience (Palmer,

Ludwig, & Stapleton, 1994). Only about *one-half* of all students who attend community colleges with *aspirations to attain a baccalaureate degree* will actually *make the transition to 4-year institutions*—with or without an associate degree (American Council on Education, 1991; Pincus & Archer, 1989; Watkins, 1990). During the 1980s, 75% of full-time first-year students in public community colleges indicated a desire to obtain a bachelor's degree—however, the actual transfer rate ranged from 15 to 25 percent; overall, no more than *20-25 percent* of community college students who *aspired to earn a bachelor's degree ever did so* (Pincus & Archer, 1989). This disturbing discrepancy has been referred to as the *"baccalaureate gap"* (American Council on Education, 1995).

(4) Attention to closing this gap between 2- and 4-year institutions has important implications for promoting *underrepresented* students' *access* to, and *achievement* of the baccalaureate degree. Disproportionately large numbers of underrepresented college students attend community colleges. The majority of first-generation college students begin higher education at 2-year institutions (Rendon, 1995; Richardson & Skinner, 1992), and are overrepresented at these institutions (Striplin, 1999). However, the transfer (access) rate of *minority students* from 2- to 4-year institutions is significantly *lower than that for majority students* (Angel & Barrera, 1991), despite the fact that (a) the degree aspirations of minority students are very similar to those of majority students (Center for the Study of Community Colleges, 1985; College Entrance Examination Board, cited in Richardson & Bender, 1987), and (b) the majority of first-generation students realize the importance of a bachelor's degree for upward mobility (London, 1996).

Listed in this section of the taxonomy (subsection 5.1) is a series of 2- and 4-year college collaborative practices that have promise for promoting successful transfer among community college students in general, and underrepresented students in particular. Following these practices is a listing of collaborative strategies designed to promote collaboration among 4-year institutions (subsection 5.2).

• MAJOR FORMS OF *INTER-INSTITUTIONAL* COLLABORATION

5.1 Collaboration Between *2-year* & *4-year* Colleges

• *Course articulation agreements,* a.k.a., *transfer articulation agreements* (*TAGS*) between 2- and 4-year colleges to facilitate a "seamless" transfer transition. (These agreements can becommunicated in paper or on line, the latter being posted on the internet for easy access and retrieval.)

• *Guaranteed Transfer* (a.k.a., *"2 + 2 Agreements"*) between 2- and 4-year colleges which ensure acceptance of community-college transfer students and their transfer credits at the collaborating 4-year college or university.

• *Inverted Degree* Models: certain vocational/technical programs at the 2-year college are followed by a special general education sequence offered by the 4-year college that culminates with a baccalaureate degree.

• *Inter-Institutional Transfer Councils/Offices/Committees* designed to facilitate transfer by conducting regularly scheduled meetings between 2- and 4-year college representatives in specific program areas or academic disciplines.

• *Partnerships Grant* Programs: 2- and 4-year colleges jointly write grants that provide fiscal support for collaborative efforts between the two institutions (e.g., Ford Foundation grants sponsored by the American Council on Education).

• Two-year institutions host a *college fair* at which 4-year college admission representatives staff information tables and answer transfer-related questions for potential transfer students.

• Two-year college publishes *transfer newsletter* and 4-year institutions are invited to submit announcements and spotlights.

• Four-year college permits neighboring 2-year college students to *access its facilities* (e.g., library, computer services, athletic events).

• *Four*-year colleges offer *courses* to nearby *community college students* (either on their home campus or at the university campus) so that potential transfer students can obtain *advanced transfer credit*.

• *Cross-registration* program in which 2- and 4-year colleges collaborate to allow students at each institution to enroll in courses offered at the other college.
• Two-year college partners with university to offer *bachelor's, master's or Ph.D. degree programs at the 2-year college campus* so that students are able to pursue advanced degrees without having to travel to a different campus.
These programs are designed for two major purposes: (a) to accommodate students who live at great distance from university campuses, and (b) to provide efficient and cost-effective education for students preparing to enter career fields that have drastic shortages of professional personnel (e.g., teaching, nursing, technology).

- *College visits* by 2-year college students to 4-year institutions—which provide them with a *campus tour* and opportunities to meet with transfer orientation professions and departmental advisors.

- *Advisors* of 2-year college students and 4-year college *admission officers* collaborate to *identify and recruit* potential transfer students (e.g., underrepresented students).

- Two-year college provides 4-year colleges with a *directory of transfer-ready minority students.*

- Four-year college *earmarks transfer-student grants/ scholarships* specifically for students transferring from neighboring 2-year colleges.

- *Transfer-student orientation* programs sponsored by 4-year colleges for potential or just-admitted transfer students.

- *Mentoring* relationships between 4-year college *faculty* and 2-year college *students* that are designed to assist transfer students' eventual *transition* to the 4-year institution.

- *Major-specific workshops* provided by 4-year college faculty for 2-year college students interested in pursuing popular and competitive fields of study (e.g., business, engineering, pre-med).

- Two-year and four-year college *faculty* combine to *teach* courses in a "summer bridge" program for *transfer students* who are transitioning from the 2-year to 4-year institution (e.g., a college success course).

5.2 Collaboration Among *4-year Institutions*

• Consortium of colleges formed to facilitate institutional *assessment* via mutual data-sharing, non-competitive *peer comparisons*, and *benchmarking* of most effective practices.

One ambitious illustration of this strategy is the "Restructuring for Urban Student Success" (RUSS) project, a national-level collaborative funded by The Pew Charitable Trusts, in which a consortium of urban public universities develop approaches to improving performance and retention of urban college students (particularly fist-year students), and explore ways to assess those approaches. A culminating project associated with this program is for institutions to electronically display assessment results of effective practices on Web-based "institutional portfolios" which member institutions can navigate and emulate. (This electronic component of the program is referred to as the *Urban Universities Portfolio Project* or *UUPP*.)

• Consortium of colleges formed to encourage resource sharing and *reduce operating costs*, or to alleviate the deleterious effects of inter-institutional competition (e.g., nearby colleges pool money to reduce the travel costs of an outside speaker; racially homogeneous colleges collaborate to recruit students and faculty that are underrepresented at their home institutions).

• *Technology-Based Distance Learning Collaborative*: A consortium of small colleges employs *compressed video technology* to create a learning environment that allows each individual campus to expand its resources *by tapping the resources of all member institutions*.

This technology enables each small college to: (a) expand its curriculum by allowing its students to experience courses taught at member institutions via distance learning, (b) combine low course enrollments across member institutions offering the same course to create a class size large enough to prevent course cancellation, and (c) optimize institutional investment in new faculty by selectively recruiting and hiring faculty whose area of expertise complements or adds to that of faculty already in the consortium (e.g., hiring a new faculty member with expertise in medieval history to complement faculty at member colleges whose specializations focus on other historical periods).

• *Cross-Registration* Programs (a.k.a., *Visiting Student* Programs): students *enroll in courses at other colleges* that are not offered at their home institution, thus providing them with a wider range of curricular choices and learning experiences.

• Temporary inter-institutional *exchanges of college personnel*: for example, historically black college and a college with a disproportionately low number of African-American employees exchange faculty, staff, or administrators to promote professional development and cultural diversity on their respective campuses.

• *Summer Research Opportunities Program (SROP)*: an academic consortium of universities designed *to increase the number of minority faculty*, in which minority students are recruited from the consortium institutions to participate in *summer research projects with faculty mentors*.

6. INTER-SEGMENTAL COLLABORATION

(Collaboration Across Different Segments or Sectors of the Educational System)

Reform agents argue that there are inter-segmental gaps in the American educational pipeline which need to be bridged before the system can function in a seamless fashion. Postsecondary institutions, in particular, have tended to function independent of, rather than interdependently with other segments of the educational system. Higher education has been criticized for operating as an "isolated island" and for sitting "alone atop the educational pyramid," while condescendingly shifting blame to the K-12 sector for failing to academically prepare students for college-level work (The Pew Higher Education Roundtable, 1993, p. 9A). According to Derek Bok, Harvard president emeritus, "Very few institutions have given much encouragement to faculty interested in improving the schools. What we have done instead is simply to relegate all of the work on schools to the faculty of education, then to stuff the faculty of education down at the bottom of the campus hierarchy and ignore it. I think it would be easier to argue that we are part of the problem than it would be to argue that we are part of the solution" (1992, p. 19).

In 1983, the American Council on Education and the Education Commission of the States issued an influential national report titled, *One Third of a Nation*, which issued seven major challenges to our educational system, one of which was for its leaders to cooperate across all levels of education—from elementary through graduate school. During the 1990s, the American Association for Higher Education (AAHE) made school/college collaboration a key focus point of its national reform agenda (American Association

---

for Higher Education, 1993). These national reform efforts fueled a proliferation of school-college partnerships during the 1990s. These partnerships focused primarily on the following collaborative initiatives: (a) early identification and intervention programs in which K-12 students are brought to college campuses for educational enrichment and academic skill building, (b) professional development opportunities for college faculty and academic support professionals to engage in K-12 service and scholarship, and (c) school-college course articulation and curriculum development (Wilbur & Lambert, 1995). Specific school-college collaborative practices designed to implement these goals and other objectives relating to the school-to-college transition are included in this section of the taxonomy (subsection 6.1).

A second important inter-segmental transition in American higher education is that from undergraduate to graduate education. One particularly positive byproduct of greater collaboration between these two sectors would be improved minority accesses to graduate school and more effective recruitment of minority graduate students to faculty positions in higher education. The scope and urgency of this issue is well articulated by Ernest Boyer, "Concerns about tomorrow's professoriate cannot be seriously raised without focusing, with special urgency, on minority faculty, since the next generation of scholars will be challenged, as never before, by diversity in the classroom. The intolerably small pool of qualified minority applicants represents a shocking weakness, if not an indictment, of American education at all levels (1991, p. 66).

Another potential benefit of undergraduate-graduate school collaboration would be improved insight into the nature of the student transition between these two sectors of higher education. Historically, there has been a dearth of research on factors influencing student *access to* graduate school (Malaney, 1987) and *persistence at* graduate school (Tinto,

1993). There is little research available to answer such important questions as: (a) How well are undergraduates prepared for the graduate school experience? (b) What common adjustments need to be made by first-year graduate students to meet the distinctive demands of graduate education? (c) What characteristics of both the undergraduate and graduate experience serve to increase student persistence to graduate degree completion?

Collaborative research between undergraduate colleges and graduate schools could help answer these questions and, in so doing, may help identify solutions to the particular shortage of doctoral candidates pursuing academic careers in certain fields (e.g., science, math and technology), as well as the general shortage of minority students in graduate educational tracks leading to professorial positions in higher education (Hoffman, 1993).

Collaboration between these two sectors may also serve to enrich the preparation of graduate students because undergraduate colleges can provide graduate students with a career-relevant context for experiential learning within which they may acquire and develop student-centered professorial skills relating to teaching, advising, counseling, and mentoring. Collaboration between graduate school and undergraduate colleges might be able to provide graduate students with opportunities to develop instructional skills while under the guidance of experienced undergraduate faculty (e.g., in mentor-protegee team teaching arrangements). Such an arrangement may serve to address the 30-plus published reports calling for reform of graduate education, all of which have emphasized the need to provide greater preparation for undergraduate teaching (Nyquist, et al., 1999).

In this section of the taxonomy (subsection 6.2), a series of practices are cited whereby undergraduate colleges and graduate schools collaborate to promote undergraduate students' interest in, preparation for, and transition to graduate

education (particularly among students who have been historically underrepresented in the graduate school population).

• MAJOR FORMS OF *INTER-SEGMENTAL* COLLABORATION

6.1 Collaboration Between *Schools & Colleges,* a.k.a., *School-College Partnerships*

• *Academic Alliances*: faculty from colleges and high
schools who teach in the *same academic discipline* collaborate to identify critical *subject-matter knowledge, core concepts, and pedagogical strategies* that promote student learning in their particular subject area. (For example, high school-
and college faculty collaborate to develop subject-specific
capstone courses for high school seniors).

• *High School Outreach Programs*: colleges collaborate with high schools to facilitate high school students' *college access, transition, and retention*. These programs are often aimed at underrepresented students; if they are targeted
for younger students (e.g., students in junior high or elementary school), they are typically referred to as "*Early Identification Programs.*"
Types of High School-Outreach & Early-Identification
Practices/Programs:

• College administers *Math and English placement tests*
to high school students during the *sophomore or junior* year,
enabling teachers to work on specific elements of students'
skill development before they graduate.

• "Summer High School Juniors Program": college offers summer programming for high school *juniors* to prepare them for their senior year, their upcoming college-application process, and their eventual freshman-year experience in college.

• High school students *tutored by college students* in subject matter relating to their academic major—for purposes of promoting high school students' (a) level of academic achievement, (b) preparation for college and (c) interest in attending college.

• College provides a *teaching-learning "hotline"* for use by local high school students and high school instructors (e.g., math education hotline).

• An outstanding *high school teacher* on sabbatical leave serves as the "master learner" in a *federated learning community* model offered at a college or university.

This procedure is identical to the FLC previously described in section 1.6; the only difference being that a high school instructor, rather than a college faculty member, attends the federated courses and serves as the master learner. The high school teacher is granted a complete tuition waiver by the college—which also helps the high school pay for the instructor's replacement.

One major objective of this practice is to provide high school teachers with a professional development opportunity that may serve to enhance their ability to prepare high school students for the academic expectations and responsibilities they will encounter in college.

• College provides *feedback to high schools* on their graduates' collegiate performance—e.g., their first-year academic achievement (GPA) and retention rate.

- *University faculty* teach advanced college-credit courses to *high school seniors* for the purpose of stimulating their interest in and recruitment to college. (Note: High school students may take these course on the college campus–where they may also be allowed free access to the university's educational and recreational facilities, thereby further promoting their identification with and involvement in the college community.)

- *College students* teach one or two *lessons in a public high school*, using material from courses they are currently taking at the university. High school instructors may request topics from a menu sent to them by the college, and the college instructor awards credit to the student (e.g., extra credit; exemption from an exam or paper).

- Local high school students, faculty, and staff are invited to *college programs and special events free of charge*.

- "College Scouts Plan": *college alumni* register at the state's public libraries, and high school students are matched with these alumni to form *mentor-protegee* pairs.

- Joint high school and college *"outstanding teacher" award ceremonies*—designed to recognize outstanding secondary and postsecondary teachers, promote school-college relations, and stimulate high school students' interest in attending college (and, perhaps, pursuing a future teaching career).

- Selected *high school counselors* work with *college freshmen*, with the participating college and high school sharing the cost of these counselors' salaries. After spending two full terms on the college campus, the counselors return to their local school districts better equipped to assist high school seniors' transition to college and well prepared to train other counselors.

• *Summer Bridge* Program: High school faculty collaborate with college faculty to teach in a summer program for students who are transitioning from their last (spring) semester in high school to their first (fall) semester in college, thus serving to "bridge" students' transition from high school to higher education.

These programs typically target academically "at-risk" students (e.g., low-income, first-generation, underrepresented students), include an orientation to higher education and a residential experience–whereby participants take courses together and reside on campus in the same college residence.

• Qualified high school students are allowed to take college courses for which they receive a*dvanced college-placement credit.*

• College faculty or academic support professionals meet with teachers and counselors from feeder high schools to *review the academic performance of the school's graduates during their freshman year at the college.*

• *College of education faculty* collaborate with *high school and elementary school teachers to* identify the knowledge, professional skills, and personal qualities associated with *effective K-12 instruction*, for the purpose of improving teacher education and preparation.

• High school and college collaborate to offer an *academic track for academically-advanced high school students*, enabling them to *complete both high school and college in six years*—through a curriculum jointly developed and taught by high school and college faculty.

- *"2+2" or "2+1" arrangements*: technical studies programs begun in high school are completed at a 2-year college, either as part of a certificate program or associate degree (A.A./A.S.) program.

6.2 **Collaboration between** *Undergraduate* **Colleges & *Graduate/Professional* Schools**

- Graduate students *teach or team-teach* undergraduate courses (e.g., freshman seminar).

- Graduate students in the field of counseling serve as *counselors* for undergraduate students (e.g., as part of a graduate student's internship experience).

- Graduate student serves as *advisor or mentor* to undergraduates who may be interested in pursuing graduate work in the same academic discipline as that of the graduate student.

- Undergraduates serve as *research assistants* for graduate students (e.g., assisting graduate research relating to a master's or doctoral thesis).

- Provision of *summer research assistantships* for selected *undergraduates* to work with *graduate faculty* (e.g., to promote minority student interest in and preparation for graduate school).

- *Senior-year experience* programs designed jointly by undergraduate and graduate faculty in order to facilitate students' *transition from undergraduate to graduate education.* (For example, programs linking college seniors with beginning graduate students in the same academic field in order to stimulate undergraduate interest in pursuing graduate studies and to facilitate the application-and-transition process.)

• To help college graduates who encounter a *tight job market*, the university allows its spring baccalaureate-degree graduates to continue their studies in graduate school at *special alumni tuition rates.*

• Undergraduates who complete their baccalaureate degree in good academic standing are allowed to enter the school's graduate program to earn an *accelerated (one-year) master's degree—tuition-free*—if they maintain good academic standing.

• *Dual Degree* Program (a.k.a., *Grow Your Own* Program): students are accepted into a bachelor and master degree program *simultaneously* and are *automatically* granted admission to the graduate program if they complete the undergraduate program in good standing.

• *Combined B.S.-M.S. programs* that enable students to earn *both degrees in five years* (e.g., engineering, physical therapy).

• *Doctoral-Loan Incentive* Programs: college graduates are offered "loan forgiveness," whereby their loan converts to a grant if they enroll in and complete a doctoral degree, then return to the doctorate-granting college as a full-time faculty member. (Most often, these programs are targeted for groups who are underrepresented among college faculty— e.g., racial/ethnic minorities, women, and disabled students.)

7. COLLEGE-COMMUNITY COLLABORATION

(Collaboration Between Colleges and Corporations, Non-Profit Organizations, or Citizens in the Local Community

Most college faculty have never worked outside of academe and, therefore, may know little about the public or private sectors for which they are preparing the vast majority of college graduates (The Pew Higher Education Roundtable, 1994). Moreover, most colleges and universities do not know how their "products" (graduates) actually perform in the workplace (Seymour, 1993). Conversely, many business executives and corporate recruiters do not fully understand or appreciate the goals and curriculum of higher education, particularly general education and the liberal arts (Jones, 1985).

Thus, greater communication and collaboration between these two parties could pay rich dividends in terms of reducing the mismatch between the college experience and the realities of the contemporary work world. For example, both colleges and corporations could work together to enhance the career relevance of the college curriculum via faculty-executive exchanges and jointly conducted research on the initial work adjustments and subsequent career development of college graduates. Such partnerships may also reap economic benefits for both parties: Businesses might profit through reducing the cost of running the "hidden university"—the estimated 40 billion dollars which corporate America spends annually on workforce education (Cross, 1985). Colleges, in turn, could profit from corporate redirection of workforce education costs to support ongoing, industry-linked curriculum development and faculty development (Alfred & Hilpert, 1985).

Other members of the local community with whom postsecondary institutions may collaborate include non-profit organizations and local citizens. Qualitative research on postsecondary institutions with exceptional records and reputations for involving students actively in the college experience indicates that one of their distinguishing characteristics is the number of partnerships they have formed with community organizations. These partnerships allow their students to capitalize on the surrounding geographical setting to create meaningful off-campus learning opportunities that are consistent with the college mission (Kuh, Schuh, & Associates, 1991). While students benefit from community-based experiential learning, they also benefit community organizations by bolstering their workforce and service staff without incurring increased labor costs.

Reciprocally, citizens in the local community can provide service to the college, both inside the classroom (e.g., as guest speakers) and outside the classroom (e.g., as advisors or mentors). The authors of a national report issued by the Association of American Colleges (1988) point out that community members are a rich and underutilized source of educational support who are often very willing and able to assist college students, "Many effective people in the community outside the college have great interest in being close to students, but colleges rarely take initiative to seek them out. Affiliates may be given an honorific title, such as Fellow or Mentor. They will not only come to the campus but also invite students into their homes and introduce them to their community, business, or professional associates and activities, thus strengthening the students' sense of the world beyond the campus" (p. 47).

Listed in this section of the taxonomy are specific practices demonstrating collaboration between the college and local community, all of which have the potential for serving the needs of both parties while simultaneously promoting harmonious "town-gown" relations.

• MAJOR FORMS OF *COLLEGE-COMMUNITY* COLLABORATION

7.1 Collaboration between *Colleges* and *Corporate Organizations*

• Corporations provide college students with off-campus, *work-based learning experiences in the form of part-time employment* or academic *credit-bearing internships.*

• Corporations provide college students with opportunities for *shadowing* (a.k.a., "externships"), whereby students are given the opportunity to "follow around" practicing professionals and observe the nature of their work for a short period of time—typically 1-3 days.

• *Cooperative Education* (a.k.a., *Cooperative Work/ Study*): programs that enable college students to *alternate periods of academic study with periods of employment*, typically in job related to the student's major field of study. Most often these programs are structured so that the baccalaureate degree is completed in five years.

• Corporations provide *career mentors* for college students.

• *Executive-in-Residence* Program: experienced business executive lives in a student residence where s/he mentors students, and teaches business courses or seminars.

• *Faculty development* programs in which corporate professionals and faculty members attempt to promote "positive transfer" between students' present *academic* experience in their major and their *work* experience in corporate organizations.

• *Inter-organizational exchanges* between college faculty or staff and corporate professionals designed to promote mutual understanding and appreciation of their respective practices. (For example, college releases a business faculty member to work in a private company in exchange for use of a corporate executive).

• Business professionals serve on *college* advisory committees, while faculty serve on *corporate* advisory committees.

• *Corporate-College Alliances*: university-business partnerships in which businesses benefit from the research capacity of universities, while the university benefits from (a) development of closer connections between its business curriculum and the work world, (b) establishment of new internships or job sources for its students, and (c) increased revenue generated by programs jointly developed with corporations (e.g., corporation and university develop a potentially profitable new-executive development program).

• *Industry-University Research Collobaratives*: college faculty and corporate researchers join forces to empirically investigate issues of mutual concern and common interest. (For example, research projects conducted jointly by faculty and business professionals to identify characteristics of college graduates who display successful career performance during their first year of employment).

• *Senior-year experience* courses designed collaboratively by college faculty/staff and corporate professionals for the purpose of facilitating graduating students' *transition* from *college* to *career*.
For example: (a) senior courses in which potential employers and alumni from different career fields serve as guest speakers or as resources for out-of-class projects; (b) "linked" courses in the senior year designed to integrate theory and practice—such as an internship experience and senior seminar taken concurrently—that is jointly designed to include coordinated content and mutually reinforcing assignments.

• Corporations provide *fiscal support for college publications* through paid advertising (e.g., to support publications costs of a campus newspaper or college yearbook).

• College and local corporations collaborate to *reduce the cost of a college education* for *low-income* students (e.g., jointly sponsored scholarships, or stipends for purchase of books and other auxiliary educational expenses).

• Corporation *subsidizes its employees* for enrollment in college courses and/or completion of a college degree program.

7.2 Collaboration between *Colleges* and *Non-Profit Organizations or Citizens in the Local Community*

• *Community-Based Learning*: local organizations provide *volunteer* opportunities or *service-learning* experiences that are relevant to students' academic major and also meet the needs of the community. (For example, college recommends outstanding political science majors for participation in a community-based, legislative internship program.)

• College selects outstanding *elementary education stu-*

dents to serve as *mentors* for at-risk children in *public housing communities.*

• *Juvenile offenders* in the local community are matched with and mentored by selected *college students*—who receive training for their role and stipends or partial scholarships for their service.

• College-to-Community *Referral Systems*: college provides students with referrals to local community services. (For example, adult students are referred to child-care providers in the nearby community, or to the community's Adult Learning Center for low-cost courses in writing or math that will prepare them for college-level work).

• College collaborates with *landlords* in the local community to provide students with viable off-campus housing opportunities (e.g., college provides landlord with computers for renting students that can be linked to the university's system; landlord provides rent reductions for students who achieve academic excellence).

• *Action Research* (a.k.a., *Participatory Research* or *Practitioner Research*): faculty work jointly with community members to conduct *research in the local community* that is designed to address *practical* problems or issues of current and mutual concern.

• Faculty are granted *sabbatical leaves* for extended, intensive contact with *practicing professionals* in the local community (especially professionals working in fields that are undergoing rapid and radical change).

• College invites community members to attend *campus programs* and *special events* free of charge.

• College invites *senior citizens* in the community to take *courses*, either for credit or to audit, at reduced or no cost.

• College offers *free tuition* for *unemployed* residents in the local community, or allows them to fill up seats in any classes that are under-enrolled without a fee.

• College offers *career transition workshops* and or *career counseling services* to assist adults in the community who are presently *unemployed* or are in the process of *changing jobs*.

• *Public officials* serve as *visiting lecturers or guest speakers* in courses that relate to their area of expertise (e.g., political science, criminal justice, or human services).

• *Retired teachers* in the local community observe and coach *student teachers*.

• Community volunteers serve as *mentors or tutors* for college students (e.g., members of the Service Core of Retired Executives mentor college seniors majoring in business).

• Members of the community serve as *external, "third-party" evaluators* of student performance—e.g., employers assess students' job-application performance during mock interviews.

• *Minority-Student Mentorship* Programs: minority professionals in the community serve as mentors to minority students enrolled in college.

One successful illustration of such a program is the "EN-LACE Program" (a.k.a., "Puente Project"), whereby Hispanic professionals in the local community are linked to Hispanic college students' classroom learning experiences. For example, on writing assignments in certain courses, students work with a mentor whose profession is related to the student's academic major or career interests.

- *Community Compacts for Student Success (CCSS)*(a.k.a., "K-16 Councils"): college engages *urban community leaders* to work together with *local school system* and *local businesses* for a 6-8 year period to create systemic reforms that are designed to increase the number of *economically disadvantaged* and *underrepresented* students who complete high school, enter higher education, and persist to baccalaureate degree completion.

- *College-Church* Collaboratives: Local church groups collaborate with colleges to promote the *educational advancement* of congregational members. For example, church leaders work with college admissions staff to share information on the advantages of college with high school students and parents in congregations with high proportions of minority students).

A more elaborate illustration of this form of collaboration is the *Interdenominational Churches for Educational Excellence (ICEE)*, a partnership between a consortium of inner-city black congregations in Indianapolis and Indiana University–Purdue University at Indianapolis. The major objective of the consortium is to promote interest in college among secondary and elementary school students through such activities as: visits to campuses and museums, science and math study sessions on Saturdays, and weekend stays in college residences

Conclusion

One subtle but potentially powerful byproduct of the formidable array of collaborative practices cited in this taxonomy is that they model for students—in visible and multiple ways—how their college enacts its espoused ideal of *community* and puts it into actual practice. As Suzanne Morse (1989) points out in her review of the literature on preparing college students for successful citizenship, "These lessons show the importance of community and politics in context. Students, like all people, learn from the community in which they live. The challenge is to structure the college environment like a community with shared interests" (p. 94). If the college itself is not a model of community, it is in no position to advocate or educate for community (American Association for Community and Junior Colleges, 1988). When colleges fail to do so, Tompkins (1992) describes the consequences: "If institutions that purport to educate young people don't embody society's cherished ideas—community, cooperation, harmony—then what young people will learn will be the standards the institutions do embody: competition, hierarchy, and isolation" (p. 15).

By observing and directly experiencing how colleges operate, what its most esteemed members value, and how members of the college community relate to each other, students learn what really matters most—and these informal lessons are likely to have more impact on them than what is formally taught in the curriculum. The power of such informal observational and experiential learning has long been noted in the scholarly literature, and has been labeled "collateral learning" (Dewey, 1938), the "hidden curriculum" (Snyder, 1971) and, most recently, the "implicit curriculum" (Astin, 1988). Alexander Astin notes that higher education's informal curriculum needs major modification if it expects its students to learn to collaborate and to value community:

"Undergraduates' values and belief can be shaped by a wide variety of institutional policies and practices that are largely independent of the content of the formal curriculum These polices and practices can adversely affect students' ability to work cooperatively with peers and to develop a sense of trust within organizational settings. The implicit curriculum, at least as it is manifested in the typical undergraduate program today, is not designed to foster such qualities. On the contrary, it seems more likely to encourage competitiveness, individualism, and a relative lack of interest in co-workers and in organizational goals" (1988, p. 10).

If colleges and universities were to intentionally and comprehensively implement the collaborative practices identified in each major domain of the proposed taxonomy, then the adverse effects of higher education's traditional "implicit curriculum" would be redressed and replaced by an informal curriculum that models cooperation, collaboration, and community.

References

Abercrombie, M. L. J. (1960). *The anatomy of judgment.* New York: Hutchinson.

Adelman, C. (1998). What proportion of college students earn a degree? *AAHE Bulletin, 57*(2) pp. 7-9.

Alfred, D., & Hilpert, J. M. (1985). The liberal arts and the personnel needs of complex organizations. *Liberal Education, 7*(1), 61-76.

American Association of Community and Junior Colleges (1988). *Building communities: A vision for a new century.* A report of the Commission on the Future of Community Colleges. Washington, D.C.: National Center for Higher Education.

American Association for Higher Education (1993). Organizing for learning. *AAHE Bulletin* (September), p. 6.

American Association for Higher Education (1993). AAHE's new agenda on school/college collaboration. *AAHE Bulletin, 45*(9), pp. 10-13.

American College Personnel Association (1975). A student development model for student affairs in tomorrow's higher education. *Journal of College Student Personnel, 16*, 334-341.

American College Personnel Association (1994). *The student learning imperative: Implications for student affairs.* Washington, D.C.: Author.

American Council on Education (1991). *Setting the national agenda: Academic achievement and transfer.* National Center for Academic Achievement & Transfer. Washington, D.C.: Author.

American Council on Education (1995). *Campus trends, 1994.* Washington, D.C.: Author.

Amir, Y. (1969). Contact hypothesis in ethnic relations. *Psychological Bulletin, 71(5)*, 319-342.

Arciniega, T. A. (1990). The nature and importance of minority leaders in the decade ahead. *AAHE Bulletin, 42*(10), pp. 10-14.

Aronson, E., Blaney, N., Stephin, C., Sikes, J., & Snapp, M. (1978). *The jigsaw classroom.* Beverly Hills, CA: Sage.

Association of American Colleges (1985). *Integrity in the curriculum: A report to the academic community.* Washington, D.C.: Author.

Association of American Colleges (1988). *A new vitality in general education: Planning, teaching, and supporting effective liberal learning by the task group on general education.* Washington, D.C.: Author.

Association of American Colleges (1990). *The challenge of connecting learning: Project on liberal learning, study in depth and the arts and science major.* Washington, D.C.: Author.

Astin, A. (1975). *Preventing students from dropping out*. San Francisco: Jossey-Bass.

Astin, A. W. (1977). *Four critical years: Effect of college on beliefs, attitudes, and knowledge*. San Francisco: Jossey-Bass.

Astin, A. W. (1988). The implicit curriculum: What are we really teaching our undergraduates? *Liberal Education, 74*(1), 6-10.

Astin, A. W. (1991). *Assessment for excellence*. New York: Macmillan.

Astin, A. W. (1993). *What matters in college? Four critical years revisited*. San Francisco: Jossey-Bass.

Astin, A.W., & Associates (1996). *The American freshman: National norms for fall 1995*. Los Angeles: Higher Education Research Institute, University of California, Los Angeles.

Austin, A. E., & Baldwin, R. E. (1991). *Faculty collaboration: Enhancing the quality of scholarship and teaching*. ASHE-ERIC Higher Education Report No. 7. Washington D.C.: The George Washington University.

Austin, A. E., Rice, E. R., Splete, A. P. & Associates (1991). *A good place to work: Sourcebook for the academic workplace*. Washington, D.C.: The Council of Independent Colleges.

Banta, T. W., Lund, J. P., Black, K. E., & Oblander, F. W. (1996). *Assessment in practice: Putting principles to work in college campuses*. San Francisco: Jossey-Bass.

Bargh, J., & Schul, Y. (1980). On the cognitive benefits of teaching. *Journal of Educational Psychology, 72,* 593-604.

Barr, M. J., & Upcraft, M. L. (Eds.)(1990). *New futures for student affairs: Building a vision for professional leadership and practice.* San Francisco: Jossey-Bass.

Barrera, A., & Angel, D. (1991). Minority participation in community colleges: A status report. In D. Angel & A. Barrera (Eds.), *Rekindling minority enrollment* (pp. 1-4). New Directions for Community Colleges, no. 74. San Francisco: Jossey-Bass.

Beagle, R. & Johnson, C. M. (1991, March). *Minority exposure to corporate America (MECA): Enhancing business and organizational career success.* Paper presented at the Second National Conference on The Senior Year Experience, San Antonio.

Benware, C. A., & Deci, E. L. (1984). Quality of learning with an active versus passive motivational set. *American Educational Research Journal, 21*(4), 755-765.

Bok, D. (1992). Reclaiming the public trust. *Change, 24*(1), pp. 12-19.

Bonsangue, M. V. (1993). The effects of calculus workshop groups on minority achievement in mathematics, science, and engineering. *Cooperative Learning and College Teaching, 3*(3), pp. 8-9.

Boyer, E. L. (1987). *College: The undergraduate experience in America.* New York: Harper & Row.

Boyer, E. L. (1991). *Scholarship reconsidered: Priorities of the professoriate.* Princeton, NJ: Carnegie Foundation for the Advancement of Teaching.

Boyer, E. L. (1992, February). *Keynote address.* Delivered at the 11th Annual Meeting of the Freshman Year Experience, Columbia, South Carolina.

Brower, A. M. (1997). Prototype matching for future selves: Information management strategies in the transition to college. *Journal of The Freshman Year Experience & Students in Transition, 9*(1), 7-42.

Brower, A. M., & Dettinger, K. M. (1998). What is a learning community? Toward a comprehensive model. *About Campus, 3*(5), pp. 15-21.

Buckley, F. J. (1999). *Team teaching: What, why, and how.* San Francisco: Jossey-Bass.

Burke, J. C., Modarresi, S. & Serban, A. M. (1999). Performance: Shouldn't it count for something in state budgeting? *Change, 31*(6), pp. 17-23.

California Community Colleges (1994). *Transfer education.* Sacramento, CA: State Chancellor's Office.

Carnegie Foundation and The American Council on Education (1989). *National survey of college and university presidents.* Washington D.C.: Authors.

Carter, D. J., & Wilson, R. (1995). *Minorities in higher education.* Washington, D.C.: American Council on Education.

Center for the Study of Community Colleges (1985). *Transfer education in American community colleges.* Los Angeles: Ford Foundation.

Chickering, A. W. (1969). *Education and identity.* San Francisco: Jossey-Bass.

Chickering, A. W., & Gamson, Z. F. (1987). Seven principles for good practice in undergraduate education. *AAHE Bulletin, 39*(7), pp. 3-7.

Cooper, J. L. (1997). New evidence of the power of cooperative learning. *Cooperative Learning and College Teaching, 7*(3), pp. 1-2.

Cross, K. P. (1985). Education for the 21st century. *NASPA Journal, 23*(1), 7-18.

Cross, K. P. (1998). Why learning communities? Why now? *About Campus, 3*(3), pp. 4-11.

Cuseo, J. B. (2001). *Igniting student involvement, peer interaction, and teamwork: A taxonnomy of cooperative learning structures and collaborative learning strategies.* Stillwater, OK: New Forums Press.

Daly, W. T. (1992). The academy, the economy, and the liberal arts. *Academe, 78*(4), 10-12.

Davis, J. R. (1995). *Interdisciplinary courses and team teaching: New arrangements for learning.* San Francisco: Jossey-Bass.

Dewey, J. (1938). *Experience and education.* London: Collier Books.

Education Commission of the States (1986). *Transforming the state role in higher education.* Denver, CO: Author.

Edwards, R. (1999). The academic department: How does it fit into the university reform agenda? *Change, 31*(5), pp. 16-27.

El-Khawas, E. (1987). Colleges reclaim the assessment initiative. *Educational Record, 68*(2), 54-58.

Endo, J., & Harpel, R. (1982). The effects of student-faculty interaction on students' educational outcomes. *Research in Higher Education, 16,* 115-138.

Engelkemeyer, S. W., & Brown, S. C. (1998). Powerful partnerships: A sharedresponsibility for learning. *AAHE Bulletin, 51*(2), pp. 10-12.

Epper, R. E. (1999). Applying benchmarking to higher education: Some lessons from experience. *Change, 31*(6), pp. 24-31.

Ewell, P. E. (1994). An analyst's view. *Change, 26*(6), pp. 24-29.

Ewell, P. T., & Boyer, C. M. (1988). Acting out state-mandated assessment. *Change, 20 (4)* pp. 41-47.

Finklestein, M. J. (1984). *The American academic profession.* Columbus, Ohio: Ohio State University Press.

Friedlander, J. (1980). Are college support programs and services reaching high-risk students? *Journal of College Student Personnel, 21*(1), 23-28.

Gabelnick, F., MacGregor, J., Matthews, R. S., & Smith, B. L. (1990). *Learning communities: Creating connections among students, faculty, and disciplines.* New Directions for Teaching and Learning, No. 41. San Francisco: Jossey-Bass.

Gardner, P. D., & Lambert, S. E. (1993). It's a hard, hard, hard, hard, hard, hard world. *Journal of Career Planning and Employment, 53*(2), 41-49.

Gilbert, S. W. (1995). Technology and the changing academy: Symptoms, questions, and suggestions. *Change, 27*(5), pp. 58-61.

Giles-Gee, H. F. (1994). Creating a new vision of articulation. *AAHE Bulletin, 47*(4), pp. 6-8.

Green, M. G. (Ed.)(1989). *Minorities on campus: A handbook for enhancing diversity.* Washington, D.C.: American Council on Education.

Haylock, K. (1996). Thinking differently about school reform: College and university leadership for the big changes we need. *Change, 28(1)*, pp. 13-18.

Hoffman, N, (1993). Shifting gears: How to get results with affirmative action. *Change, 25*(2), pp. 30-34.

Holton, E. F. III (1995). College graduates' experiences and attitudes during organizational entry. *Human Resource Development Quarterly, 6*, 59-78.

Holton, E. F. III (1998). Preparing students for life beyond the classroom. In J. N. Gardner, G. Van der Veer, & Associates, *The senior year experience: Facilitating integra-*

tion, reflection, closure, and transition (pp. 95-115). San
Francisco: Jossey-Bass.

Hord, S. M. (1981). *Working together: Cooperation or collaboration. Austin: University of Texas at Austin, Research
and Development Center for Teacher Education.* (ERIC
Document Reproduction No. 226 450)

Institute for Research in Higher Education at the University
of Pennsylvania (1996). Leaving hats at the door: Themes
from the Pew Campus Roundtables. *Change, 28*(3), pp.
51-54.

Johnson, D. W., Johnson, R. T., & Smith, K. A. (1993). Structured controversy/constructive controversy. *Cooperative
Learning and College Teaching, 3*(3), pp. 14-15.

Johnson, D. W., Marujuama, G., Johnson, R., Nelson, D., &
Spon, L. (1981). Effects of cooperative, competitive, and
individualistic goal structures on achievement: A meta-
analysis. *Psychological Bulletin, 89(1),* 47-62.

Johnson, W. B., & Packard, A. H. (1987). *Workforce 2000:
Work and workers for the 21ˢᵗ century.* Indianapolis, IN:
Hudson Institute.

Johnson, K., Sulzer-Azaroff, B., & Mass, C. (1977). The effects of internal proctoring upon examination performance
in a personalized instruction course. *Journal of Personalized Instruction, 1,* 113-117.

Jones, T. B. (1985). Liberal learning and business study. *Liberal Education, 7*(1), 61-76.

Kagan, S. (1992). *Cooperative learning.* San Juan Capistrano: Resources for Teachers.

Kagan, S. (1998). Teams of four are magic! *Cooperative Learning and College Teaching, 9*(1), p. 9.

Knapp, J. R., & Karabenick, S. A. (1988). Incidence of formal and informal academic help-seeking in higher education. *Journal of College Student Development, 29(3)*, 223-227.

Kuh, G. D. (2001). Assessing what really matters to student learning: Inside the National Survey of Student Engagement. *Change, 33*(3), pp. 10-17, 66.

Kuh, G. D., & Banta, T. W. (2000). Faculty-student affairs collaboration on assessment: Lessons from the field. *About Campus, 4*(6), pp. 4-11.

Kuh, G. D., Schuh, J., Whitt, E., & Associates (1991). *Involving colleges: Encouraging student learning and personal development through out-of-class experiences.* San Francisco: Jossey-Bass.

Lasher, H., & Brush, C. (1990, March). *Enhancing "success behavior skills" perceived as relevant and necessary for effectiveness in the business environment: An innovative capstone learning approach.* Paper presented at the First National Conference on The Senior Year Experience, Atlanta.

Leibowitz, Z. B., Schlossberg, N. K., & Shore, J. E. (1991). Stopping the revolving door. *Training and Development Journal, 45*(2), 43-50.

Levine, A., & Cureton, J. S. (1998). Collegiate life: An obituary. *Change, 30*(3), pp. 12-17.

Levitz, R. (1992). Minority student retention. *Recruitment & Retention in Higher Education, 6*(4), pp. 4-5.

London, H. B. (1996). How college affects first-generation students. *About Campus, 1*(5), pp. 9-13, 23.

Malaney, G. (1987, November). *A decade of research on graduate students: A review of literature in academic journals.* Paper presented at the meeting of the Association for the Study of Higher Education, Baltimore, MD.

McCloskey, D. N. (1991). Invisible colleges and economics: An unacknowledged crisis in academic life. *Change, 23*(6), pp. 10-12

McConahay, J. B. (1981). Reducing racial prejudice in desegregated schools. In W. D. Hawley (Ed.), *Effective school desegregation: Equity, quality, and feasibility* (pp. 35-53). Beverly Hills, CA: Sage.

McKeachie, W. J., Pintrich, P., Lin, Y., & Smith, D. (1986). *Teaching and learning in the college classroom: A review of the research literature.* Ann Arbor: University of Michigan, NCRIPTAL.

Meiklejohn, A. (1932). *The experimental college.* New York: Harper & Row.

Miller, T. K., & Prince, J. S. (1976). *The future of student affairs.* San Francisco: Jossey-Bass.

Millis, B. J., & Cottell, P. G., Jr. (1998). *Cooperative learning for higher education faculty*. Phoenix, AZ: American Council on Education and The Oryx Press.

"Minorities in the Sciences: What went wrong?" (1994). *Access, 2*(1), pp. 1, 3, & 6.

Morse, S. W. (1989). *Renewing civic capacity: Preparing college students for service and citizenship*. ASHE-ERIC Higher Education Report No. 8. Washington, D.C.: The George Washington University, School of Education and Human Development.

National Center for Education Statistics (1993) *Trends in academic progress*. Washington, D.C.: Department of Education, Office of Educational Research and Improvement.

National Endowment for the Humanities (1984). *To reclaim a legacy: A report on the humanities in higher education*. Washington, D.C.: Author.

National Institute of Education (1984). *Involvement in learning: Realizing the potential of American higher education* (Report of the NIE Study Group on the Condition of Excellence in American Higher Education). Washington, D.C.: U.S. Government Printing Office.

Nyquist, J.D., Manning, L., Wulff, D. H., Austin, A. E., Sprague, J., Fraser, P. K., Calcagno, C., & Woodford, B. (1999). On the road to becoming a professor: The graduate student experience. *Change, 31*(3), pp. 18-27.

Orfield, G. (1993). Federal policy and college opportunity: Refurbishing a rusted dream. *Change, 25*(2), pp. 10-15.

Palmer, J. C., Ludwig, M., & Stapleton, L. (1994). *At what point do community college students transfer to baccalaureate-granting institutions? Evidence from a 13-state study.* National Center for Academic Achievement & Transfer. Washington, D.C.: American Council on Education.

Pantages, T. J., & Creedan, C. F. (1978). Studies of college attrition: 1950-1975. *Review of Educational Research, 48,* 49-101.

Parnell, D. (1986). *The neglected majority.* Washington, D.C.: Community College Press.

Pascarella, E. T., & Chapman, D. W. (1983). Validation of a theoretical model of college withdrawal: Interaction effects in a multi-institutional sample. *Research in Higher Education, 19(1),* 25-48.

Pascarella, E. T., & Terenzini, P.T. (1991). *How college affects students: Findings and insights from twenty years of research.* San Francisco: Jossey-Bass.

Pincus, F. L., & Archer, E. (1989). *Bridges to opportunity: Are community colleges meeting the transfer needs of minority students?* (Research report). Academy for Educational Development and College Entrance Examination Board. New York: CEEB.

Rendon, L. I., & Garza, H. (1996). Closing the gap between two- and four-year institutions. In L. I. Rendon & R. O. Hope (Eds.), *Education for a new majority: Transforming America's educational system for diversity* (pp. 289-308). San Francisco: Jossey-Bass.

Richardson, R. C., & Bender, L. (1987). *Fostering minority access and achievement in higher education.* San Francisco: Jossey- Bass.

Scott, D. K., & Awbrey, S. M. (1993). Transforming scholarship. *Change, 25*(4), pp. 38-43.

Senge, P. M. (1994). *The fifth discipline: The art and practice of the learning organization.* New York: Doubleday.

Seymour, D. (1993). Quality on campus: Three institutions, three beginnings. *Change, 25*(3), pp. 14-27.

Shapiro, N. S., & Levine, J. H. (1999). *Creating communities: A practical guide to winning support, organizing for change, and implementing programs.* San Francisco: Jossey-Bass.

Slavin, R. E. (1990). *Cooperative learning: Theory, research, and practice.* Englewood Cliffs, NJ: Prentice Hall.

Smith, J. B., Walter, T. L., & Hoey G. (1992). Support programs and student self-efficacy: Do first-year students know when they need help? *Journal of The Freshman Year Experience, 4*(2), 41-67.

Snyder, B. R. (1971). *The hidden curriculum.* New York: Knopf.

Stodt, M. M. & Klepper, W. M. (Eds.). (1987). *Increasing retention: Academic and student affairs administrators in partnership.* New Directions for Higher Education. San Francisco: Jossey-Bass.

Stoecker, J., Pascarella, E. T., & Wolfle, L. M. (1988). Persistence in higher education: A 9-year test of a theoretical model. *Journal of College Student Development, 29(3)*, 196-209.

Striplin, J. J. (1999, June). *Facilitating transfer for first-generation community college students.* ERIC Clearinghouse for Community Colleges. University of California at Los Angeles, Los Angeles, CA. (EDO-JC-99-05)

Taylor, M. S. (1988). Effects of college internships on individual participants. *Journal of Applied Psychology, 73(3)*, 393-401.

Terenzini, P. T. (2000, May 30). *First invited presentation to the First-Year Assessment (FYA) Listserv.* Retrieved from the World Wide Web: http://www.brevard.edu/fyc.

The Pew Higher Education Roundtable (1993). A transatlantic dialogue. *Policy Perspectives, 5*(1), pp. 4A-11A.

The Pew Higher Education Roundtable (1994). Voices. *Policy Perspectives, 5*(3), pp. 1B-3B.

Tinto, V. (1993). *Leaving college: Rethinking the causes and cures for student attrition* (2nd ed.). Chicago: University of Chicago Press.

Tobias, S. (1990). *They're not dumb, they're different.* New York: Norton.

Tompkins, J. (1992). The way we live now. *Change, 24*(6), pp. 12-20.

Treisman, P. U. (1985). A study of the mathematics performance of Black students at the University of California,
Berkeley (Doctoral dissertation, University of California,
Berkeley, 1986). *Dissertation Abstracts International, 47,*
1641-A.

Upcraft, M. L., & Schuh, J. H. (1996). *Assessment in student
affairs: A guide for practitioners.* San Francisco: Jossey-
Bass.

Volkwein, J., King, M. C., & Terenzini, P. T. (1986). Student-
faculty relationships and intellectual growth among transfer students. *Journal of Higher Education, 57,* 413-430.

Walter, P. H. (1988). The professor as specialist and general-
ist. *Academe, 74*(3), 25-28.

Whitman, N. A. (1988). *Peer teaching: To teach is to learn
twice.* ASHE-ERIC Higher Education Report No. 4. Washington, D.C.: Association for the Study of Higher Education.

Wiener, H. S. (1986). Collaborative learning in the classroom:
A guide to evaluation. *College English, 48(1),* 52-61.

Wilbur, F. P., & Lambert, L. M. (Eds.)(1995). *Linking
America's schools and colleges* (2nd ed.). Washington D.C.:
American Association for Higher Education.

Wilson, R. C. (1975). *College professors and their impact on
students.* New York: Wiley and Sons

Wingspread Group. (1993). *An American imperative: Higher
expectations for higher education.* Racine, WI: The Johnson
Foundation.

Worchel, S. (1979). Cooperation and the reduction of inter-group conflict: Some determining factors. In W. Austin & S. Worchel (Eds.), *The social psychology of intergroup relations.* Monterey, California: Brooks/Cole.

Organizing to Collaborate